Weddings
A Family Affair

The New Etiquette for Second Marriages and Couples with Divorced Parents

Margorie Engel

foreword by

Beverly Clark

WILSHIRE PUBLICATIONS

WILSHIRE PUBLICATIONS
1120A Mark Avenue
Carpinteria, CA 93013
(800) 888–6866

Publisher's Cataloging–in–Publication
(Provided by Quality Books, Inc.)
Engel, Margorie Louise.
Weddings, a family affair : the new etiquette for second
marriages and couples with divorced parents / Margorie Engel ;
foreword by Beverly Clark. – 1st ed.
p. cm.
Includes index.
"previously published as Weddings for complicated families
. . . 1993"–T.p. verso.
ISBN: 0–934081–16–6
1. Wedding etiquette. 2. Remarriage. I. Title.
BJ2065.R44B64 1998   395'.22
QBI97–41424

Printed in the U.S.A.

10 9 8 7 6 5 4 3 2 1

Book Design—Penelope C. Paine
Text Editor—Gail Kearns
Typesetting & Book Layout—Cirrus Design
Cover Art & Illustrations—Itoko Maeno

To my daughters, Beth and Jenny

With much love,

Mom

MARGORIE G. ENGEL

My mother is an artist. Her drawing of the path through the woods is my reminder that sometimes it is necessary to go outside the lines in order to achieve the goals you want in life.

When planning your own wedding in a complex family, I suggest to you that it is necessary to go outside the lines of rigid convention in order to discover harmony.

Margorie Engel

Foreword

Even under the most traditional of circumstances, putting together a perfect wedding requires a great deal of energy and planning. When you consider that 90 percent of American families are made up of divorced parents, remarried parents, stepchildren, half siblings, and significant others, it becomes apparent that most families do not fit our outdated notion of "traditional". Nearly half of all brides ages eighteen to twenty-six have divorced parents and one third of all brides have been married before. Clearly, there is a fundamental shift in the wedding demographics of our society.

Besides this, there is a trend toward bigger and more elaborate weddings. No longer embracing the small, intimate ceremony of recent years, more and more couples are choosing large weddings and inviting an average of 200 guests. Undoubtedly these celebrations will require intricate guidelines for putting it all together. I have heard many stories, good and bad, from brides, families, and the wedding professionals who assist them. Couples are searching for ways to bring their unique families together and strengthen the bonds that bind them as a unit.

I first experienced this when planning my own wedding. My parents were divorced and my father had remarried. I wanted to make sure that everyone felt relaxed and comfortable and could fulfill the responsibilities that came with being a member of the bridal party. Unfortunately, Margorie Engel had not yet written this book; I certainly could have used it!

I am now delighted to be able to lend my support and encouragement to Margorie Engel on the publication of this book, *Weddings: A Family Affair.* I think you will enjoy her sensibility and humor as she lays down some guidelines and solutions. Hopefully our combined stories and know-how will provide valuable suggestions, insights and ideals that you can use in your circumstance.

As you plan your wedding, gather those happy moments around you and celebrate the traditions, both old and new, that you have chosen. This is a day for your whole family to celebrate, a day for fond memories and new hopes, not just for you, but for all those who love you.

Beverly Clark

Prologue

For years, my daughters, Beth and Jenny, and I have communicated via little messages and letters we call "kitchen table notes". This practice began during my hectic single-parent days when the three of us left notes for each other on the kitchen table.

When two of my three step-daughters, Wendy, Hollie and Candi, were ready to plan their weddings, I scrambled for guidelines to help our family avoid difficult or explosive situations. I read whatever I could find—etiquette books, bridal magazines and wedding planning guides. I discovered the expertise of many wedding suppliers and consultants, along with insights from family counselors, clergy and step-family organizations.

It soon became clear that I could help other complex families avoid turmoil and confusion with a book that especially addresses weddings and divorce. Beth and Jenny suggested that I write this book to all brides and grooms as if I were writing to them in our kitchen table notes.

I interviewed many family members as well as brides and grooms. I discovered that the unusual is really the usual and that whatever might happen during the planning of any wedding has probably already happened to another couple. Many of the people with whom I spoke, consciously or unconsciously identified potential upsets long before they became a problem. Happily, most of these couples remain married today and their relatives are still talking to each other, proving that with some care and concern it is possible to include all the family in the wedding affair.

This book is about the common problems and challenges of planning a wedding for a complex family. Just seeing an assortment of options may inspire you to come up with solutions that are uniquely suited to your own circumstance, ways that will help you and your family create a special, wonderful wedding day.

My best wishes,
Margorie Engel

CONTENTS

Great Beginnings

For Couples with Divorced Parents

Happy Endings

For Couples Planning a Second Marriage

The New Etiquette

The experience of planning a wedding in America today is radically different from what it was just a generation ago. Parent–child relationships have changed, family structure has been reshaped by divorce, and the customary repertoire of wedding etiquette no longer applies. Emotional ambivalence and social ambiguity undermine the old rules.

Families tend to see the problems as overwhelming. Planning a wedding doesn't have to be that way. I have found that social mores for weddings after a divorce are gradually developing. There are ways to rescue order from the jaws of chaos. As my husband, Steve, says, when seeking practical answers for wedding decisions, "KISS" (Keep It Simple, Sweetheart).

Great Beginnings

For Couples with Divorced Parents

Getting Started

Your vision of how your wedding should be probably began when you were a young girl. You've had additional years to be programmed through novels, movies, and magazines. The media helped to create a fantasy for you and the fantasy has become the model for what you hope will become a reality.

The dream–come–true versions of the wedding can be easily orchestrated by Hollywood but mere mortals are in for a stressful period. Fantasy and reality part company for almost every bride. The vision can be further complicated by a divorce. Nowadays, families with a divorce or two in the past, and some extra parents, through remarriage, in the present, need a guidebook to get them through the maze.

More important than simply correctness, the happiness and warmth of the event are the ultimate wedding goal. A beautiful bride can become frayed around the edges if she forgets that the main purpose of a wedding is to create a new family, not to destroy the old ones. Forget about what might have been, "If only mom and dad hadn't divorced." Your family has been restructured and that fact has put you in the position of making some fundamental choices.

It is an autobiographical fact that you are a child with divorced

While visualizing your wedding day, remember that it's what you do ahead of time, and how you do it, that sets the tone. The wedding is not just the event itself but the whole process of preparing for it, experiencing it, and finally taking your new position in society.

parents. Your wedding may be coming up before you and your family have figured out exactly when and where you can and can't relate comfortably with each other. Wedding planning may be a perilous time. Are you going to focus on the limitations or the possibilities?

Accent the Positive

Children sometimes feel that their lives are overshadowed by their parents' divorce. They feel that they don't get the kind of attention that they imagine children from intact families take for granted. Divorce stole the spark from wedding activities for bride Bobbi who was convinced that, "All of these planning problems are because my parents are divorced." She focused on the limitations.

Bride Sylvia felt totally alone because she assumed that, "These things don't happen in a conventional family." But she decided that she couldn't do things differently until she saw things differently. So Sylvia intentionally focused on the possibilities.

I know that you want a beautiful and dignified wedding. It's a wonderful goal. How do you get there?

There are very few "musts" for a successful wedding, but, when there is a divorce/remarriage in the family history, understanding the importance of respecting everyone's feelings and being receptive to developing new wedding "customs" are both admirable things to do.

Getting Your Act Together

Although each family pretty much muddles through on their own, I did discover plenty of people who were remarkable in their ability to successfully juggle time, money, emotions, and human resources while coordinating wedding details. Today, with the birth of the Internet, more and more resources have become available on-line. Some of them are professional wedding planners whose styles range from businesslike to grandmotherly.

According to a bridal magazine, the average American wedding now costs about $16,000. The wedding consultant business is growing, in part because families hope and pray to avoid costly mistakes. Divorced families are also grateful for the buffer provided by an experienced outsider. You can call the Association of Bridal Consultants for referral to a member near you.

Leslie, a bridal consultant, told me that over 60 percent of her clients were either children of divorced parents or had, themselves, been through a divorce.

I was particularly touched by one paragraph in bridal consultant Jan's response to my query for success stories. She wrote, "This may sound strange, but I really do pray for the couple as well as the family members all the while I am coordinating their wedding . . . and for any of the challenges that may come up during any part of the celebration. It really does work!"

With divorced parents, years of tradition are not there to draw upon. I've seen young couples abandon familiar wedding rituals altogether. Others rework those rituals to address perceptions, feelings, and interactions among family members. They take the opportunity to outline a new family structure, if only for the ceremony and the reception.

Association of Bridal Consultants
200 Chestnutland Road
New Milford, CT 06776
tel: 860-355-0464
fax: 860-354-1404
www.bridalnet.com/abc
E-mail:
BridalAssn@aol.com

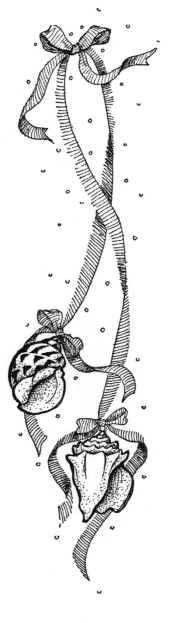

Avoiding Pitfalls

Weddings provide an occasion for drawing together or an opportunity for emotional warfare. I've heard war stories about individuals who had an emotional investment in hostility and a deep inner need to complain. I've watched people spend the entire wedding planning period being openly, genuinely and perfectly obnoxious. Excuses range from, "That woman (stepmother) stole my husband," to a father expressing fury at the family minister who befriended his ex-wife during the divorce proceedings.

Your wedding day can lose its celebration flavor if there is a struggle for control or the exclusion of one of your parents. While parents are busy setting up their control maneuvers through money or refusing to cooperate, I've seen brides and bridegrooms try to "get back at a parent." They do this by excluding a mother or father from any significant role in the wedding.

If you're leaning in the direction of exclusion, are you making the decision with a vindictive spirit or for truly appropriate reasons? Not too many eyebrows will be raised if a parent is excluded because he or she left when you were an infant and virtually all contact has been lost through the years. You're going to find understanding in cases of known abuse as well. These are extreme examples but you get the point.

When a mother or father has given neither emotional nor financial support for many years, in addition to the fact that the bride or groom may not want to have anything to do with that parent, I see no reason to insist that the parent be invited to participate in the wedding.

I have very negative feelings toward parents who make promises they don't keep or who treat their parenting responsibilities very lightly. I think these parents have disqualified themselves from worthwhile parent privileges. On the other hand, no parent is perfect . . . If you can summon forgiveness, your wedding may be part of the family healing process.

In either event, consider your choices and motives carefully. You will live with the consequences for a very long time. Remember, your goal is to have a beautiful wedding—after all, it's just a few hours—not to even the score for a lifetime of unresolved issues.

Is Anybody Grown Up?

Possibly not. Nevertheless, everyone's job is to show a measure of dignity. Make an effort to use the wedding as a family coming together. Sometimes a big common objective—the wedding for a son or daughter—makes healing a possibility when an ordinary day is powerless.

Adults do have an amazing way of being, well, adult. Avoid automatically expecting the worst. Negative expectations can inadvertently help create problems where none would have otherwise existed. Even with a history of animosity or indifference, parents aren't always unbearably uncomfortable being "together for our children's special occasions."

One set of parents, the Cobbs—married for over twenty-six years, separated for six years, and divorced just prior to their daughter's wedding—actually functioned throughout the planning and wedding day as if they were still married to each other. In this case, I'm sure it helped that neither parent had a "significant other" at the time of their daughter's wedding.

Rising to the Occasion

I continue to hear wonderful success stories about family members who use the wedding planning period for some serious introspection. Families grow up during these months of discussions between mothers and fathers, stepmothers and stepfathers, and their sons and daughters:

- Communication between ex-spouses is renewed

- Negative energy is refocused in more positive ways

- Friends who are in the other person's shoes share what it feels like to be on the other side

- Preconceived notions are abolished

Martha, a wedding caterer, told me about divorced clients who met with her jointly, shared decision-making and expenses, and were generally very cordial throughout the planning process. Having experienced a bitter divorce herself, she said she was absolutely sure she couldn't do it that way. Fortunately, Martha's anticipation anxiety is fairly low because she has two sons!

You'll need to communicate with members of your extended family (grandparents, aunts, uncles, cousins) if you want to elicit supportive behavior. Because these people don't always live close by, they haven't had the opportunity to see how relationships have shifted and settled during the period after a divorce. Tell them about the (hopefully) positive changes. If they don't realize that the war is over, they may continue to throw other people's spitballs based on an outdated and possibly more negative picture.

Insensitivity among family members is an old story. This is one of those circumstances where you may feel more adult than the adults. Simply remember, you are just as related to everyone in your extended family as you ever were. Difficulties they have with the other side of your family are really their problem, not yours.

Degrees of Civility

Brides and bridegrooms use the terms "friendly" and "not friendly" to describe the relationship between their divorced parents. No matter how difficult the planning period may be, during the wedding festivities your parents will probably be on their best behavior. The guests may not be aware of tensions even though the couple may feel every nuance, real or imagined. That's to be expected. The objective is the appearance of civility if not cordiality.

Do not confuse this objective with trying to get your parents back together. Weddings have a way of bringing back this longing, no matter how old sons and daughters have become. Trying to force something that is usually impossible will only make things worse. Deep down, you know that wishing doesn't change things. Make the time to think about, and accept, reality.

Your parents' demeanor may range anywhere from "not a jealous bone . . . " to "psychosclerosis" (hardening of the attitudes), and your job is to help them overlook certain behaviors or events *and* to avoid potential problems. If this is too large a burden for you alone, ask an aunt or uncle or whoever functions as your family's practical mediator to help you handle your parents. There is such a thing as a dignified agreement to maintain distance between family members who do not get along.

If the child in you is thinking, "Why can't my parents put aside their hard feelings and do it just for me?" try to understand the power of emotions and look at the situation from their point of view. Accepting your parents as individuals, each with their strengths and limitations, can advance your own growth toward adult relationships.

Bride Carla told me that her fiance's stepmother sat the young couple down and "chewed us out" for bad-mouthing his birth mother. She admitted that the couple responded to this by subsequently ignoring the stepmother and lavishing attention on the mother. However, the story ultimately had a happy ending when the young people made time to sort out their feelings. They rebuilt their bridges about a year after the wedding.

If you're backing yourself into this kind of corner, remember that the words, "I'm sorry," have opened many communication doors.

Balance, harmony, and good manners. That's what this book is all about. Goodwill and kindness is summed up in bride Julie's comment: "It made me so happy to see my divorced parents talking together so nicely."

The anticipation of coming into contact during the wedding festivities allows parents to think about what relationship statement they want to enact. Most divorced parents, happily or grudgingly, try very hard to be amiable throughout the wedding activities. If you remember that they are not really required to spend a lot of time with each other, you can all follow the Golden Rule for High-Stress Weddings:

"Everyone should concentrate on helping the Bride and Groom plan a wonderful wedding day."

Remember, dearest bride, this includes you too! Life is a two-way street, give and take, as they say.

When the wedding has been successfully
navigated, everyone involved will probably
feel a sense of relief from the stress and
anxiety. Congratulations will be in order
for all of the participants who are defining
new territory.

Matrimonial Chessboard

Far and away the most frequent confusion is about what to do when there are "too many" parents at the wedding.

As children from the divorce boom era, you're on the leading edge of change in the dynamics of family rituals. You're shaping views of relationships, moral standards, and expectations of parents, family, and spouses. For the time being, however, there are no hard and fast rules.

Stepping Stones

For wedding planning purposes, stepparents seem to be the family members with "boundary problems." They have very high visibility for being recognized as "In" or "Out" of the family emotional system. When they're "In," everybody knows it because plans are discussed with them and they are asked to participate. When they're "Out," they're really "OUT!" They are ignored (benign neglect or deliberate exclusion?) and left to fend for themselves around family ritual times. The absolute minimum honor you must do a stepparent is to recognize your stepparent's existence and to recognize your stepfather's position as a husband and your stepmother's position as a wife.

Weddings are about love. The bride and groom love each other and their love radiates out to encompass the whole family. Try working on the principle that there's enough love to go around and that it's impossible to give or receive too much love. Cast your net as widely as possible. That philosophy may allow everyone to participate with grace.

I've observed that brides and grooms are usually receptive to the idea of "many parents." When a parent remarries, children seem to add the new parent without subtracting the one that was there before. The added parent simply goes into a new slot.

Parents can be more difficult, however. Divorced mothers and fathers may use various methods to keep their original position intact and to control the wedding. Adult children tell me that money and guilt trips are the most effective. Subtle warfare and even out–and–out verbal attacks have been the methods of choice for the purpose of classifying the other side as "Out" of the family.

Bride Dianne's mother was furious with Dianne's father for saying that he would pay for her wedding only if he and his new wife could make all of the arrangements with the bride and groom. They did not want to share the experience with her mother at all. Dianne was expected to choose between loyalty to her mother and money to pay wedding bills.

A gathering of the clan in this milieu is emotionally and socially symbolic because it formalizes family connections in a public way. Brides and grooms tell me that the second child's wedding, in the divorced family, is always easier. That first reworking of formal family patterns opens up new possibilities, good and bad, yet oftentimes creates successful expanded relationships.

Weddings are about love. The bride and groom love each other and their love radiates out to encompass the whole family. Try working on the principle that there's enough love to go around and that it's impossible to give or receive too much love. Cast your net as widely as possible. That philosophy may allow everyone to participate with grace.

Successful family integration stories are bountiful. Weddings provide a socially acceptable opportunity for all members of the extended family to be in the same place at the same time. They may have avoided contact before because of tension or anger, but the wedding is of common and positive interest.

Stepmother Elaine described seven out of eight biological and stepchildren's weddings as "going off without a hitch." The eighth wedding (after being a stepparent for 24 years) was an "emotional disaster." One of the stepdaughters and her birth mother planned a wedding that did not include any of Elaine's children (the bride's step siblings) on the invitation list.

Expect the Unexpected

The brides and grooms who contributed ideas for this book invariably told stories about stepmothers and stepfathers who failed to live up to their mean-spirited fairy tale reputations. The length of family relationship is certainly a factor, but not always meaning that short equals "so-so" and long equals "good" relations.

At the other extreme, several brides told stories about how their fathers' girlfriends were the support system for understanding the parental conflicts and for helping to brainstorm possible solutions. In Jo's story, her father had agreed to pay for the reception and then became furious at the number of guests from her mother's side. The ultimate decision was to have multiple smaller reception parties in several geographic areas so they could share the wedding cheer with friends and relatives unable to travel long distances to the ceremony. Each party had its own local family member as host/hostess.

Bride Debbra described very mixed feelings about her new stepmother because her stepmother's relationship with her father began before her parents' divorce. Her mother had no desire whatsoever to share the limelight with her successor. Debbra cautiously approached her stepmother to discuss her own feelings as well as her mother's fears that the stepmother would try to usurp the "mother-of-the-bride role" throughout the wedding day. When she learned, firsthand, that her stepmother could empathize with the tension and visualized her role as "very quietly supportive," plans began to proceed smoothly.

In my interviews, I heard many stepmothers and stepfathers described positively:

> one stepmother tried to recognize how the bride's mother was feeling.

a stepfather made it very clear that the bride's birth parents should be able to run the show.

another stepmother played a pivotal role in resolving problems.

another stepmother was a very "low key" hostess. For instance, she was not with her stepdaughter when the bridesmaids and the bride were getting dressed; her mother was.

I also heard stories about stepparents who felt that the tension was sufficiently thick to warrant bowing out of the wedding ritual altogether. Did they reach this decision in order to spare the child or to spare themselves? A bit of both, probably. I wonder about the effects of this exclusion on the future relationship between stepparents and the newlyweds.

Now, to be perfectly honest, it is also true that hundreds of parents and stepparents have let loose with off–the–wall behavior at some point during wedding festivities. You might feel that all of your arrangements have "gone to smash." On the other hand, unexpected mishaps can certainly make for a memorable wedding day. Try to keep a sense of humor!

Wedding Checklists

The following checklists are adapted from Beverly Clark's *Planning a Wedding to Remember*. They help you organize your time and activities. These are general recommendations and can be changed to suit your particular needs.

Bride's Checklist

Six to Twelve Months Before

- Tell all family members.
- Decide on who will be the primary sponsoring parent(s).
- Select a wedding date and time.
- Make a preliminary budget.
- Determine your wedding theme or style.
- Reserve your ceremony and reception location.
- Determine who will officiate at the ceremony.
- If desired, design a wedding ceremony to include family members.
- Hire a wedding consultant, if you plan to use one.
- Decide on your color scheme.
- Determine the size of the guest list.
- Start compiling names and addresses of guests.
- Select bridal attendants.
- Have fiancé select his attendants.
- Plan reception.
- Check catering facilities, if at a club or hotel.
- Select a caterer, if one is necessary.
- Select a professional photographer and videographer.
- Select a professional florist.
- Select your dress and headpiece.
- Announce your engagement in the newspaper.
- Select bridesmaids' dresses.
- Select engagement ring with fiancé, if he has not already done so.

Four Months Before

- Shop for wedding rings and other symbols of family unity.

- Make final arrangements for ceremony (deposits should be paid, contracts signed).
- Make sure all bridal attire is ordered.
- Talk to children in second/third marriages.
- Have all mothers coordinate and select their dresses.
- Register at a bridal registry in the towns of all appropriate families.
- Order invitations and personal stationery.
- Complete the guest lists and compile them in order.
- Select the men's wedding attire and reserve the right sizes.
- Check requirements for blood test and marriage license in your state.
- Make appointment for physical exam.
- Start planning the honeymoon.
- Decide where you will live after the wedding.
- Begin shopping for trousseau.

Two Months Before

- Address invitations and announcements. They should be mailed four to six weeks before wedding.
- Finalize all details with caterer, photographer, florist, reception hall manager, musicians, etc.
- Order wedding cake, if not supplied by caterer.
- Finalize ceremony details with officiant.
- Make rehearsal arrangements.
- Plan rehearsal dinner.
- Plan bridesmaids' luncheon.
- Make appointments with hairdresser.
- Arrange accommodations for out-of-town attendants, guests, and family members.
- Finalize honeymoon plans.

One Month Before

- Have a final fitting for your and bridal attendants' gowns.
- Have a formal bridal portrait done.
- Complete all physical or dental appointments.
- Get blood test and marriage license.
- Make transportation arrangements for the wedding day.
- Purchase gifts for attendants.
- Purchase gift for fiancé and/or children, if gifts are being exchanged.
- Have the bridesmaids' luncheon.
- Purchase going away outfit.
- Keep a careful record of all gifts received (write thank-you notes immediately instead of letting them pile up).
- Make sure you have all accessories, toasting goblets, ring pillow, garter, candles, etc.
- Select responsible person to handle guest book and determine its location.

Two Weeks Before

- Attend to business and legal details. Get necessary forms to change names on Social Security card, driver's license, insurance and medical plans, bank accounts; make a will.
- Prepare wedding announcements to be sent to newspaper.
- Reconfirm the accommodations for out-of-town guests.
- Arrange to have possessions and gifts moved to your new home. Give a change-of-address card to the post office.
- Finish addressing announcements to be mailed on the wedding day.

One Week Before

- Contact guests and family members who have not responded.
- Give the final count to caterer and review details.
- Go over final details with all professional services you have engaged. Inform them of any changes.
- Give photographer family information and list of pictures you want.
- Purchase cameras for tables.
- Plan toasts for reception to include family members, children, etc.
- Give the videographer a list of shots you would like included in the video.
- Give all musicians the lists of music for the ceremony and reception.
- Plan the seating arrangements.
- Plan lineup for receiving line.
- Arrange for someone to assist with last-minute errands and to help you dress.
- Practice having your hair done to make sure it comes out properly, and determine the time it will take.
- Practice using your make-up in the same type of lighting you will have on the wedding date.
- Keep up with the writing of your thank-you notes.
- Pack your suitcase for the honeymoon.
- Make sure you have the marriage license.
- Make sure you have the wedding rings, and they fit.
- Make sure all wedding attire is picked up and fits properly.
- Have a rehearsal with all participants, reviewing their duties.

- Attend rehearsal dinner party. Stay calm and enjoy yourself.
- Stay with the desired parent the night before the wedding. Get to bed early. You will want to look and feel great the next day.

On the Wedding Day

- Be sure to eat something. You have a big day ahead, and many brides have been known to faint.
- Take a nice relaxing bath.
- Fix hair or have an appointment to have it done at least three to four hours before the ceremony.
- Make sure nails are done. Allow plenty of time to apply make-up. Have all accessories together.
- Start dressing one to one-and-a-half hours before the ceremony. If pictures are being taken before the ceremony, then have yourself and attendants ready about two hours before the ceremony.
- Have the music start thirty minutes before ceremony.
- Have guests seated. Five minutes before the ceremony, have groom's parents seated. Immediately before procession, the bride's mother is seated and the aisle runner is rolled out.

After the Wedding

- Send announcement and wedding picture to newspapers.
- Mail announcements.
- Write and mail thank-you notes.

Groom's Checklist

Six to Twelve Months Before

- Tell all family members.
- Purchase the bride's engagement ring.
- Discuss with fiancée the date, type of wedding, and ceremony.
- Start on your guest list.
- Choose best man and ushers.
- Start planning and making necessary arrangements for the honeymoon.
- Discuss and plan with fiancée your new home together. If fiancée is moving in with you, start cleaning out closets, cupboards, and drawers to make room for your bride and wedding gifts.

Four Months Before

- Shop with fiancée for wedding rings and symbols of family unity.
- Complete your guest list, including full names, addresses and zip codes with phone numbers.
- Check requirements for blood test and marriage license in your state, or the state you are being married in.
- Select and order men's wedding attire with your fiancée.
- Finalize all honeymoon plans and send in deposits if required (don't delay—some resorts fill up fast in popular months).

Two Months Before

- Meet with officiant to finalize ceremony details.
- Assist parents with plans for the rehearsal dinner party.
- Discuss the amount and the financial arrangement for the flowers which are the groom's responsibility.
- Arrange accommodations for out-of-town attendants.

One Month Before

- See that all attendants have been fitted and wedding attire has been ordered.
- Purchase gifts for best man and ushers.
- Purchase wedding gift for fiancée and/or children, if gifts are being exchanged.
- Pick up wedding rings. Make sure they fit.
- Take care of business and legal affairs (add bride's name to insurance policies and medical plans, make a new will, add her name to joint checking account or joint charge cards). If you have both agreed to a prenuptial agreement, have it drawn up and signed.

Two Weeks Before

- Together with fiancée, gather necessary documents and get your marriage license.
- Arrange wedding day transportation.
- Reconfirm accommodations for out-of-town guests.
- If moving, give change-of-address card to post office; arrange to have utilities and phone service turned on in the new home. If not moving, finish cleaning and reorganizing your home; help your fiancée move her things.
- Have your hair cut.

The Week Before

- Discuss all final details with fiancée; offer to assist if needed.
- Pick up and try on wedding attire.
- See that attendants get their wedding attire.
- Pack clothes for honeymoon.
- Reconfirm all honeymoon reservations.
- If flying, make sure you have plane tickets.
- See to it that you and your attendants are at the rehearsal and they know their duties.
- Go over special seating or pew cards with ushers.
- Arrange for gifts brought to the reception to be taken to your new home.
- Make sure luggage is in the car or the hotel where you will stay your first night.
- Attend rehearsal dinner. Relax and enjoy yourself.
- Get to bed early. You want to look and feel your best!

The Wedding Day

- Be sure to eat something in the morning.
- Allow plenty of time to get dressed (start one hour before ceremony).
- Get to the ceremony location on time!
- Give the best man the bride's wedding ring.
- Place the officiant's fee in a sealed envelope. Give it to the best man so he may present it after the ceremony. Don't forget to take the marriage license to the ceremony, or make sure the best man will bring it.
- Have the best man and maid of honor sign the wedding certificate as witnesses.
- At the wedding dance first with your bride, then with all mothers and the bridesmaids.

- Just before leaving the reception, thank the bride's sponsoring parents, and say good-bye to your parents.

After the Wedding

- Make sure on the first day of the honeymoon to send flowers or a telegram expressing your appreciation and thanking all sponsoring parents again for a beautiful wedding and reception.

My most brilliant achievement was my ability to be able to persuade my wife to marry me.

— Winston Churchill

Negotiating and Working Together

When children of divorced parents announce that they are getting married, there is an implicit demand made on adults in two households to respond appropriately to their children's special celebration. The planning and execution of this ritual event will make or break multiple family relationships—for the time being or permanently.

At the moment of the announcement, individuals in an extended family are all at a "different place" in terms of acceptance, disappointment, guilt, anger, fear, and resentment. Often parents and children have been ignoring unresolved issues for years. Tolerance, if not forgiveness, can be the happy byproduct when divorced parents decide to share in the wedding planning and festivities. The requirement of all participants is a determination to cooperate in spite of the past.

This section is about ways for parents to negotiate a truce first and then together work with their offspring's other household. It's

When you make the effort to get everybody involved, family members with different interests will be encouraged to commit themselves to working together for the wedding.

The main goal for any wedding is HAPPINESS. Happiness for the bride and groom and happiness for your families, or as many of them as want to share this occasion. Happiness doesn't just happen. It needs to be lovingly and carefully cultivated.

One of my favorite stories involves a family where the mother and father could interact socially but just didn't work together very well. The bride's Dad Jim and Stepfather Richard were on the same wavelength so it was the fathers who worked out the details with the young couple.

hard work but the stories I've been told offer encouragement. A lot of families making the effort find that their anger and discomfort gradually diminish.

The Common Goal

Family groups do not work well unless the members feel that they have some input and influence over what is happening. Family members involved need to consider themselves as important participants in decisions regarding the wedding. The bride and groom are in a position to give them that feeling by drawing them into the preparations and planning. You'll find specific suggestions for doing this throughout the book.

We all greatly fear being separated from people we care about. We go to great lengths to avoid breaking valued relationships. In planning a wedding, the bride and groom are everyone's valued relationship. Most parents try to focus on this aspect and work around less savory feelings toward one or all of the other adults hovering about the wedding couple.

The biggest mistake you can make when planning the wedding is to forget what you are trying to achieve. The main goal for any wedding is HAPPINESS. Happiness for the bride and groom and happiness for your families, or as many of them as want to share this occasion. Happiness doesn't just happen. It needs to be lovingly and carefully cultivated.

Compromise is the key to a smooth planning period. Family members agree to certain trade-offs. Agreements for the wedding plans should be practical agreements. Because everyone is busy, they need to be efficient agreements as well. And, they should try to improve, or at least not harm, the relationship between family members.

I've learned that almost everyone tends to shelve unpleasant conflicts for a later time. They hope the problems will go away. As

Scarlett O'Hara put it, "I'll think about that tomorrow." Unfortunately, time alone does not eliminate most problems. Besides, if a wedding date is already set, there may not be enough time for nature to take its course.

Flexibility

Planning a wedding requires flexibility as well as compromise. Creative possibilities may come from bridal magazines, travel brochures, and especially older relatives who have experienced many wedding styles over the years.

As you pull together all the various elements of the wedding, look for what is affordable and what is personally acceptable. Find a reasonable balance between the two. Then approach family members for their ideas. Start talks with easy-to-settle, low risk matters. As you settle some of the smaller pieces of the plans, the emotionally charged big topics will be easier to manage.

Gathering information and making decisions are two separate processes. You need to gather information first. This is a good time to start a wedding file with folders for the various components. The table of contents in this book will give you folder headings. Pick up a small cardboard file box at an office supply store.

As you get ideas from wedding service providers and your family and friends, file them away until you are ready to address that topic. Decide on the general type of wedding you want and then begin to gather information. Find out about ceremony and reception locations that fit your theme. Get a ballpark figure for expenses and check out availability around the date you are considering. It won't hurt to slip all kinds of creative or unusual ideas into your files as you go. You never know; they might provide inspiration when you get stuck and, besides, you can always throw them out later.

Think about the decision-making process of each of your

Every bride and wedding planner told me essentially the same thing, "Be willing to face unpleasant matters at the start before they create even greater problems later."

One wedding planner, Claudine, advises, "Be open to new ideas to see if they can possibly fit in. I've seen some different solutions contribute greatly to the success of the day."

family members in light of these interests. Don't forget that everyone is concerned about saving face. Your job is to find a way to reconcile past words and deeds with new (and hopefully more charitable) decisions that are being made for the wedding.

What happens when you hit a snag? Put your mental finger on the place that is hurting. For instance, are your parents emotionally over their hostile divorce but embarrassed to meet because of nasty things that were said in the heat of battle? Sometimes people want to work together but don't know how to get started. The supportive role played by you and your fiancé is a key to success. Planning becomes much easier when all involved family members feel ownership of some of the ideas. Bride Joyce told me she was constantly looking for "win–win situations" as she gathered ideas from everyone.

In real life, there will always be the person whose agenda is to make life miserable for everyone. You deal with that person by asking them to participate in the wedding activities cheerfully or withdraw from the celebration altogether.

Mudslinging is a no–win situation because everyone who participates is going to get splattered. Nor is this the time to get caught up in manipulation games. If you buckle under the pressure now, you're condoning the continuation of this miserable behavior. You are far too busy planning a wedding and need to remove as much negative tension as possible. If you find that you have an impossible person in the wedding group, it may be necessary to leave him or her out of the planning. When necessary, cut your losses and move on.

Listening to the Problem

Remember that each family member has multiple interests. For the wedding, the bride and groom's interests almost always carry the most weight. However, since most weddings are a collaborative effort, many interests need to be considered.

Arguments over how things should be done are inevitably fraught with issues of loyalty and power and "correctness." It may help to keep reminding yourself that this aspect of the wedding is not unique to brides of divorced parents.

For the most part, widely practiced rituals have core activities that are generally accepted. Chances are that there will not be a problem with the basic outline of the wedding. Divorced and remarried families, however, do have increased opportunities for different interests. The idea pool of family traditions is doubled. The good news is that for every interest there usually exists several possible solutions that could satisfy it. It doesn't hurt to listen to all ideas and suggestions. Use what you like and discard the rest.

Avoiding a Free-for-All

I'm encouraging you to include all family members who have shown a genuine interest in you and your wedding. That is a gracious thing to do; it is also very practical. People who feel abused when they are left out tend to retaliate in subtle ways.

Some Concrete Suggestions

Use the information you've assembled during your fact-finding as a basic agenda for the discussion of wedding planning topics listed in this book's table of contents.

🐝 Sit on the same side of the table when you talk. (You want literally side-by-side efforts. The message here is, "We are partners, not adversaries, and we are a team working together to plan this event.")

🐝 Acknowledge the family changes. (Do not make plans based solely on the basis of how things are done in families where the parents are not divorced.)

🐝 Encourage a wide range of possible solutions to advance shared interests. (Make lists of all options, no matter how far-fetched. Encourage creativity.)

🐝 Take detailed notes.

🐝 Provide copies of notes to everyone present. (Clearly mark areas of agreement and topics still to be worked out.)

🐝 Use meeting notes as a basis for each get-together. (Review points of agreement and then move on to the thornier issues.)

Sharing Impaired

It is very easy to get trapped into old emotional patterns or become overly defensive. Here are some dangerous communication blocks:

🐝 Time problems—urgent deadlines, all-night sessions, giving up other weekend plans.

- Personality issues—walkouts, calculating delays by being late or unprepared, emotional outbursts.

- Ego confrontations—one–upmanship, attacks on integrity, playing on a sense of guilt, fault finding, personal attacks, bringing up past hurts.

At the very least, any one of these blocks may destroy hopes of teamwork for the wedding. They may also add long–lasting damage to already strained family relationships.

As you read the following chapters about planning a wedding, you will find practical ways to address these potential problems. It is not necessary to resort to "rock, paper, scissors" as the only way to settle anything of importance. There are some effective ways of handling almost any situation or circumstance. The planning period does not have to be a negative experience; it can be a time of growth and triumph for all.

It is not necessary to resort to "rock, paper, scissors" as the only way to settle anything of importance.

Great Atmosphere

If your tolerance for tension is low and you really don't see any reason to go through this rigamarole, alternatives to traditional large weddings work well when there are problems within and between households. You still have some great options.

> You can avoid the whole mess by taking a "weddingmoon." Laura and Tom combined their wedding and honeymoon by flying to a resort in Jamaica. Their travel agent took care of all the business arrangements for the wedding package.

> Ship captains can no longer perform as the wedding officiant at sea. However, many couples follow Denise and Brian's idea. They planned a cruise vacation and arranged for the ceremony to be performed by an authorized officiant at one of the

Remember, your best approach is to humor and be flexible. If one door closes, open another door that looks like it could be fun!

scheduled port landings.

Emily and Jack met with the wedding coordinator at Walt Disney World and planned a theme wedding complete with a Cinderella coach.

Or, you can divide and conquer.

Sherry and Mike had a progressive wedding by traveling to different family locations for each portion of the event. They were married in her mother and stepfather's home; the reception was held in the city where her father and Mike's parents lived. When they returned to their own home town, their best friend hosted a party so that local friends could celebrate with the bridal couple.

When the wedding march sounds the resolute approach, the clock no longer ticks, it tolls the hour . . . The figures in the aisle are no longer individuals, they symbolize the human race.

— Anne Morrow Lindbergh

Announcing the Wedding

Whether your marriage evolves from living together for a number of years or springs from a brief courtship, when your mother and father are divorced, it's hard to be totally spontaneous. Asking permission or telling the news requires coordinated planning.

If the groom-to-be wants to carry on the tradition of asking permission for your hand in marriage, he'll approach the parent that you have been closest to—usually the parent with whom you have lived. If there's any question about the "right" person, it's best to tell him.

Spreading the News!

After the affirmative answer, "Yes, I said yes, I mean yes!" it's courteous to let the bride's parents (all of them) know about the engagement first. (After all, they'll probably want to know how you plan to make it financially.) Next stop, or phone call, is to the bridegroom's parents (all of them).

When the groom's parents are divorced, the parent he lived with after the divorce is the one who makes the first call to the bride's parents. If the bride's parents are divorced, the parent she has been living with receives this call of congratulations and the first invitation to meet with the groom's family. When the bride has remained close to her other parent, he or she is also invited next to meet with the groom's parents.

Emotions and Stepping on Toes

You're about to make practical use of your high school and college psychology classes. How well do you know your family members and their ability to share? Figuring this out will remind you of kindergarten when classmates learned to either share or take turns with a favorite object. Approximately twenty years later, parents are the classmates and the bride and groom are the prize.

You don't want any of the parents to feel left out. The best way to include everyone is to arrange for the various adult combinations to meet within a relatively short span of time. You and your fiancé will be part of each gathering. Not only is this part of the ceremonial procedure but it gives you both a chance to sense how each parent would like to participate in making the wedding plans. When planning for second and third marriages, you may have to do the same for children involved, especially adult children. They will appreciate having their opinions considered and their concerns lessened.

Announcements

After you've told your family about your plans to marry, you are free to shout your news from the rooftops. Call or write to relatives and close friends and then consider announcing wedding plans in the newspaper.

The fact that your parents are divorced does not change the procedure for newspaper announcements. Whether large city papers or small town papers, all publications have their own layout style for the "Wedding Belles." Read the bridal section of papers to which you would like to send an announcement. Somewhere on those pages you'll find information ranging from the phone number to call for information to their questionnaire for preparing engagement and wedding announcements. You can also call the paper's editorial office; they will be happy to help you.

The media does not view divorce as a social stigma. Editors tell me that a divorce in the family has no bearing on when, where, or whether the announcement will run. As long as they have complete data, a daytime phone for verification, and receive the announcement within their time schedule, the announcement will go in your local paper. Large city papers such as *The New York Times* may be selective. You can get information about their current criteria by calling the society editor.

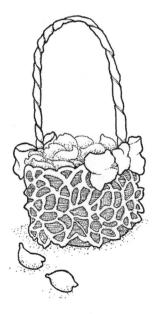

If the bridal couple (or their parents) have become prominent in the community, the paper is more likely to be interested in a full story on engagement and wedding plans, including extensive family information. Otherwise, the engagement announcement is fairly brief with names of the bride, groom, and parents. Wedding announcements often get a bit more space than those for engagements. The degree of local prominence of the members of the wedding and the size of newspaper's circulation will determine the use of photographs.

Newspaper guidelines
don't deal with the issue
of how to handle
divorced parents.

Elements of Style

The couple making the announcement usually determines the wording. Newspaper guidelines don't deal with the issue of how to handle divorced parents. Consider the following:

Do you want to use titles (Mr., Mrs., Ms.) or no titles (proper names alone)?

How many and which parents do you want to include?

Parent listing order (who's first — mother or father?)

Will you use first, middle, and last names or first and last names only?

Will a remarried mother use her given name or married name (Margaret Straus O'Brien or Mrs. Richard O'Brien)?

Draft copies of announcements using your family's names in each of the acceptable options. One of the versions will simply look better to you and also come closest to relaying your message about the formality or friendliness of family relationships. Check to find out if your parents have a strong preference.

Consistency improves writing style. For instance, if you and your parents want to use titles, then each person mentioned should have a title; if you decide to use one middle name, then each person mentioned should have their middle name in the announcement.

Doing the Honors

Etiquette encourages that engagement announcements come from the bride's side. This holds true wherever the announcements are published. In today's on-the-move society, it is not unusual for the write-ups to appear in several geographic locations—cities and towns where everyone involved is currently living. You might place announcements in the town where you and your fiancé live and work as well as in the home towns of all of your parents.

Unless your fiancé's parents are sponsoring the wedding, they are listed merely as a matter of information. When asked to describe his impression of wedding announcements and invitations, groom Woody said, "That's where you know everything about the woman's side and nothing about the man's." A possible solution to this problem of the invisible family will be discussed in upcoming chapters.

You have choices, so go with the format that feels the best to you and your parents.

The ever-growing divorce rate has produced an unprecedented number of brides and bridegrooms who have spent more years living with a stepparent than with both of their birth parents.

One Massachusetts newspaper makes engagement announcements by listing the groom's name first because "That's the form we've used for years," and "That will be the married name." This is one wedding section that bypassed the period of hyphenated surnames and hasn't noticed that many brides today are retaining their birth names after marriage.

Parents: Single, Joint, or Several

When the parents of the bride are divorced, they may still choose to make the announcement together:

> Mrs. Margaret O'Brien of New York and Mr. Jacob Straus of San Francisco, announce the engagement of their daughter, Grace Louise . . .

Typically, the announcement is made by the parent with whom the bride lives (or lived prior to moving into her own place). That parent generally has been the mother, which is why you often see announcements made by the mother—with the father mentioned in the notice:

> Mrs. Margaret Straus O'Brien of 15 Rock Glen Road announces the engagement of her daughter, Grace Louise Straus to Mr. Arthur Hamilton Jones, son of Mr. Malcolm Conrad Jones of Chicago and Mrs. Alma Jones Rizzo of Boston. Miss Straus is also the daughter of Mr. Lou Jacob Straus of San Francisco.

Although etiquette encourages acknowledging the father, this gentleman is often nowhere to be seen. Also, for personal reasons, the bride may choose not to mention her father's name.

If the mother has remarried, and the bride lived with her mother and stepfather, the parents making the announcement will most often be the mother and the stepfather. The bride's biological father is also listed. This announcement can read:

Mr. and Mrs. Richard Burr O'Brien announce the engagement of Mrs. O'Brien's daughter, Miss Grace Louise Straus to Mr. Arthur Hamilton Jones, son of Mr. Malcolm Conrad Jones of Chicago and Mrs. Alma Jones Rizzo of Boston. Miss Straus is also the daughter of Mr. Lou Jacob Straus of San Francisco.

Steps to Consider

With today's expanding families, you have another decision to include or not to include stepparents in the announcements. The latest etiquette books have not reached a consensus. Traditionally, biological parents were the only ones to make the printed news.

So, what should you do? Etiquette books have definite opinions that often differ one from the other. For the most part, newspapers have become flexible to accommodate very strong feelings that couples and their families express about announcement wording.

The ever-growing divorce rate has produced an unprecedented number of brides and bridegrooms who have spent more years living with a stepparent than with both of their birth parents. While it may be socially cumbersome, society does seem pleased to acknowledge all adults who have taken an active part in rearing a child. An expanded family announcement, when each adult has fully honored parental responsibilities, could look like this:

The engagement of Grace Louise Straus to Arthur Hamilton Jones has been announced by her parents, Mr. and Mrs. Richard Burr O'Brien of New York and Mr. and Mrs. Lou Jacob Straus of San Francisco. Mr. and Mrs. Joseph Paul Rizzo of Boston and Mr. and Mrs. Malcolm Conrad Jones of Chicago are the bridegroom's parents.

Making Choices

The prevailing philosophy at most publications is to keep doing announcements "... the same way we've always done them," unless there is a specific request to the contrary. That could mean just about anything, so inquire about what you might expect.

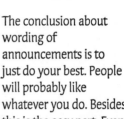

The conclusion about wording of announcements is to just do your best. People will probably like whatever you do. Besides, this is the easy part. Even more of a challenge will be how to word your wedding invitations!

Wedding Expenditures

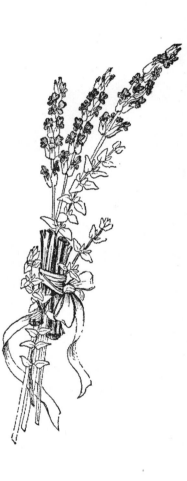

At some point in the planning stages, nearly all brides, grooms, and their respective families are torn between spending what they can reasonably afford and getting carried away. Money pressures increase as each expense is piled on. Figuring out who pays for what when your parents are divorced is seldom an ideal situation. But there are ways to make it easier on everyone. The first step is to get a clear understanding about what you are undertaking. I suggest that you stand back and look at the big picture regarding both the ceremony and the reception.

The wedding itself is actually made up of two distinct parts:

Part 1: The Ceremony

Part 2: The Reception

The wedding ceremony is a solemn family ritual. More important, it is a legally significant social contract and, very often, a religious sacrament. Your parents give their blessing by helping

Beverly says,

One stepmother I know organized a wedding for her stepdaughter and the birth mother helped with a check.

you prepare for the wedding. The state grants legal recognition through your marriage license and certificate. Your religion confers its sanction through the nuptial rite. Society acknowledges your changed status via the privileges and responsibilities accorded to a husband and wife.

. The reception is a party which celebrates the completion of a personal, social, legal, and religious passage and marks the bridal couple's entry into a new position in society.

These two parts of the wedding may be planned together or separately. Traditionally, they are planned together. I don't have to remind you that you're not in a traditional situation when you are a child with divorced parents.

Who Gets to Choose?

In real life, all weddings—not just those within divorced families—become an arena for some kind of power game. It's usually made pretty clear that whoever has the money calls the shots, including deciding whether or not to be gracious and let others make some choices. However, if one parent is paying the bill after the other parent has refused to participate, don't expect to be cheered on when inviting the non-contributing spouse and his or her companion.

The wedding couple must try to understand that after parents divorce it's not usually a case of who's right or wrong; the real issue is *who gets to choose how plans are made.* Two troublesome power dynamics can arise here. First, the parents may try to control the decision-making process. Second, the bridal couple may be offering parent wedding roles for sale. For instance, I've heard of cases where the bride said, "If you won't pay, I'll ask someone else to walk me down the aisle."

When expenses are shared by several people, everyone who

contributes wants a say in how things are done. Understanding what's going on and having a sense of humor will help get all of you through this part of the planning process. Most brides and grooms eventually find a comfort zone around the money issues.

In a divorce situation involving only biological parents, the mother and the father are equally likely to foot most of the bills.

When the father has chosen not to be part of his daughter's family picture for a very long time, the mother often assumes financial responsibility. A surprisingly large number of stepfathers make significant financial contributions to their stepdaughter's wedding—and, sadly, often get very few visible kudos in return.

If your stepfather is being emotionally and financially supportive of your wedding plans, make sure that you show your appreciation. In addition to small favors you can do, such as prepare his favorite snacks, his role as one of your parents should be acknowledged during the festivities. This can be accomplished by including him in receiving lines, by personal introductions, and, of course, in a special toast.

Most brides and grooms eventually find a comfort zone around the money issues.

With rare exceptions, the parent who contributes the cash expects and receives the most planning input and shares the final say-so with the bride and groom.

Only a Large Wedding Will Do

Before you and your parent(s) get into a huge harangue about the kind of wedding you envision, clarify the ideas and plans that are most important to you. Wedding planning books encourage you to think about wedding style (formal/casual), the type of party you're most comfortable with (intimate/large), the closest people in your life (relatives/friends/co-workers), and wedding ideas that you just can't bear to part with—at least on the first go-round.

Two volatile planning areas for most families are the size of the guest list and the style of the ceremony and reception. If you have some idea of your final objectives, it's easier to face the following facts.

🐝 After a divorce, families tend to become larger, not smaller, which results in a large guest list right off the bat.

🐝 Weddings aren't just for the starry-eyed couple. They're often showpieces for parents who feel they have something to prove in their social or business circles. When this happens, you may be thinking "small affair" while your parents are thinking "big wedding."

🐝 If you want a huge Cinderella wedding and your family can't afford it, be prepared to put off the date while you and your fiancé save up to contribute toward it. That may seem hard to do but there's a bright side: when it's your own money, there are no strings attached.

Thinking Small

You might also want to consider your future beyond the wedding day. If the real estate market where you live is favorable in terms of low prices and/or mortgage rates, you may decide to put your money toward a house rather than a large wedding. I have met many couples who chose to have a small wedding and applied their wedding money toward a down-payment. The hard part may be explaining this choice to family members who expect a big wedding.

Remember, you don't owe anyone excuses or reasons for choosing to skip the big wedding in favor of buying a house. However, from a practical standpoint, it's a good idea to speak privately with relatives who have an interest in your plans. They will be pleased by your personal attention and may also be in a position to help you financially with your house and furnishings. For instance, one couple had a garden wedding and reception at her grandparent's home in the country. Family members contributed cash toward a small home near the university where they were both members of the faculty.

It is always okay to change your childhood vision of your wedding. It is also okay to plan a wedding that is different from the kind that your relatives may expect to attend—just because family weddings have always been a certain way. This is your special day!

Who Contributes What

Divorce and economics are changing the rules. Gone are the days when only the father of the bride is expected to pick up the wedding tab. Families today are much more flexible. One bridal consultant, Peggy, guestimates that about 70 percent of weddings are paid for from multiple sources. Depending upon the financial ability of everyone who wishes to be involved, you can divide the expenses in myriad ways.

The important thing to remember is that you must have the details surrounding financial contributions ironed out before making commitments with wedding service suppliers. Even if it's possible to cancel contracts without huge penalties, you don't need the embarrassment or aggravation. Wedding planning is supposed to be fun.

There may be a number of family members who would like to help you out financially. Work your way through the list of possibilities. Jan, another bridal consultant, suggests that you write down what is promised. When you get your finances lined up, use your planning notebook to record details of the discussions and money offers. If you're really concerned about someone reneging later on, you may want to give this person a copy of your notes. On the other hand, if you've gotten a financial commitment by less than honorable means, be prepared for some repercussions.

Opening up discussions with all participating family members early on will actually take the pressure off. It's your wedding and you need to know exactly where you stand. You may need to revise plans or refigure your own financial contribution.

There are actually quite a number of ways to finance a wedding. Take a look at some of the options below:

- ❦ If the bride's mother or father is wealthy, the wealthy parent pays for everything.

- ❦ When the bride's divorced parents still have a friendly relationship, they can simply split the costs.

  They can do this equally or agree on a different split based on each parent's means. Usually, one parent assumes most or all of the planning responsibility.

- ❦ Bride's divorced parents agree to pay for everything and divide areas of responsibility and expense.

  Robin, who consults on many weddings, proposes the following example: The mother's list centers around the ceremony and includes invitations, bride's dress/veil, location, rentals, decorations, and transportation. The father's list centers around the reception and includes catering, cake, location and related rentals, music, and decorations.

- ❦ Grandparents and/or other family members step in and assume the wedding expense.

  While this option occurs more often than you might expect, it generally results in a modest, rather than lavish, wedding. After all, for most grandparents the traditional wedding was held at home—very all-in-the-family.

❦ If the bridegroom's family is wealthy (and the bride's is not), they pay for everything.

In this situation, ceremony invitations are still sent out in the bride's parents' names. The bridegroom's parents host the reception and issue those invitations. Sometimes both sets of parents consider themselves sponsors of the wedding ceremony and those invitations will reflect this by using both sets of names. See "Invitations" regarding wording of invitations.

❦ Bridegroom's divorced parents pay for wedding when bride is from overseas.

Refer to the second and the third options in which the bride's divorced parents take on the financial responsibility. It's basically the same concept.

❦ Bride's and groom's families share the cost.

This is becoming the preferred way of keeping everything fair and balanced.

Bridal consultant Toni told me that the groom's parents tend to be more involved in the planning when the bride's parents are divorced.

The offer to share the financial responsibility is extended by the groom's parents to the bride's parents. It's still considered unfashionable for the bride's parents to ask for help. If your fiancé's parents don't voluntarily come forward and he doesn't want to discuss the idea with them, move on to the next option.

🌹 "Pooled weddings."

These are paid for by a number of people including friends who volunteer and chip in for parties and even the honeymoon.

🌹 Self-funded account.

There is a definite trend in which couples are financing all or a large portion of the wedding. With the median age of brides and grooms being twenty-four and twenty-six years old, respectively, they are often more financially established than divorced parents who may be supporting a second family or living on a fixed retirement income.

🌹 Play "Chicken" and wait it out.

Jocelyn, a bridal consultant, told me that when all is said and done, if only one parent is going to help out financially, it's usually whichever parent the bride lived with after the divorce. That parent is usually the mother—the very same person who has a strong desire for her daughter to have a memorable wedding.

A number of bridal couples told me that family members liked playing a defined part in the wedding from start to finish.

For instance, Joan's mother's contribution was flowers. She participated in selecting the florist, and the color, type, and quantity of flowers, and received the bill.

At the end of the reception, Joan's mother also had the pleasure of donating the table flowers to a special cause or offering them to elderly relatives to take home as mementos.

If contributions are arriving from multiple sources, you need to be especially organized. Is all of the money going into the wedding pot, allowing the bride and bridegroom full discretion on how it is spent? Or, do specific funds come with stipulations or strings attached?

In either case, the end result is about the same. Couples know where contributors have a personal interest and make arrangements accordingly. This actually works out along the lines of a typical Spanish wedding where family and friends assume responsibility for a specific part of the wedding. For instance, one person pays for invitations, another for catering, and so on.

It's amazing how inventive and original the gestures of support can be, even from people who have very little in the way of financial resources to offer. Claudia's mother had a shoestring budget but provided hours of preliminary legwork in scoping out the best bargains. Future mother-in-law Judy attached a family heirloom veil to a handmade headpiece. Stepmother Paula made all of the catering arrangements for a reception in her home and then encouraged the bride's mother to function as hostess. Once again, I observed that the fathers' girlfriends often rallied around and provided such items as candy favors and creative table centerpieces.

Fathers, stepfathers, and grooms I meet usually play the traditional wedding role of quietly doing whatever is asked of them. They don't often come forth and volunteer to get in the middle of "women's wedding work." When given a choice, they seem more comfortable with specific chores such as ordering liquor, negotiating with limousine agencies, and making hotel arrangements for the bridal party and out-of-town guests.

So, there is a method to this madness. Weddings with the least tension seem to involve the entire "family affair" and a few "significant others." Brides and grooms who incorporate everyone with an interest in sharing the expenses of a wedding have the happiest planning period.

Meredith's father assumed responsibility for the photographer, including photographs for the bridal album as well as copies for each set of parents. He agreed to handle requests for additional photos for other family members and was reimbursed for those copies.

You don't choose your family. They are God's gift to you, as you are to them.
— Desmond Tutu

Inviting Members of the Wedding

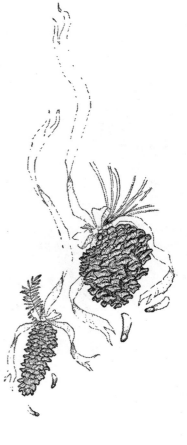

Parents are a vital element in plans for the wedding. During my interviews, I heard one statement over and over again: "Parents are supposed to be there for you to make your dream come true."

For years, divorced parents have been admonished to ignore their differences and behave in a friendly manner "just for this one special day." If they are able to put their son's or daughter's feelings ahead of their own, they are admired by all who are watching them closely. Brides and grooms often feel entitled to this courtesy. Unfortunately, I seldom hear about the young couple's responsibility to help ease a difficult situation.

And yet, the success stories I have observed are consistently the ones in which the bride and groom show sensitivity to their parents' feelings. Couples who accept the fact that they cannot act out a fairy tale version of the wedding show that they are mature enough to marry.

Mature young lovers find that they can solve most problems. Open communication, from the start, is the key. Parents' girlfriends

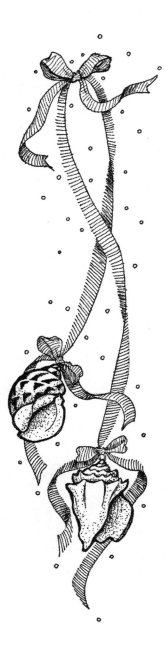

or boyfriends and stepparents often come up with viable alternatives. They care deeply about the people involved and are also able to provide some necessary distance from the emotional divorce baggage. Don't be afraid to seek their support.

Participating in the Wedding

Through the years, it has become a tradition to invite sisters and brothers to be in the wedding party. In today's complex families, this honor also goes to extended family members. The greatest compliment you can pay a "step" or half sibling is to invite him or her to be in your wedding. The gesture has brought many families together.

"My half sister was our flower girl," Joseph told me.

"My stepmother and father had been married for ten years. I asked my stepmother to do readings as part of our Catholic service so she could be part of the ceremony," John noted.

"We arranged for everyone, 'steps' and 'regular' couples, to be written into the wine ceremony at the altar," Hollie explained.

"I really like my stepsister. Of course I wanted to invite her to be in my wedding," Candi added.

When all family members who have a genuine interest in the young couple are invited to participate, the wedding can be a joyous occasion.

Bridal consultant Jan described this scene: "One of the bride's mothers giggled and giggled (she was expressing her nervousness) and said, 'What happens if I pass out?' I said, 'Good question. Would you prefer that we leave you in the aisle or should we remove your body?' She laughed and then she went down the aisle just fine."

Laughter is a great stress reliever!

The Invitation List

By now, you have a basic idea about the kind of wedding you want: small and intimate, large and formal, medium and casual—or some variation. This decision will give you a context for drawing up the guest list. For instance, "small and intimate" means just the immediate (and I mean, directly immediate) family while "large and formal" has room for your stepparents' best friends.

The wedding list is headed by the person who officiates the ceremony, witnesses/attendants, and the bride's and groom's parents (all of them, regardless of who is paying for what, unless they've been gone for so long that you don't even know them) and siblings, including steps.

If the people invited are generally considered couples, it would be a breach of etiquette to exclude spouses, fiancés, or those living together. It is not necessary to invite dates for single guests, including a parent's "casual friend." Divorced mothers and fathers sometimes grumble about this social rule. If tension is really thick, step relations and "significant others" may actually prefer not to attend.

Mothers and fathers have suffered more near-nervous breakdowns from anticipating the wedding day shared with companions of their former spouse than from any other parenting experience. Once again, however, success stories abound that tell of weddings where everything worked out fine.

Divorced parents confronted with their successor feel a challenge to their self-confidence. Divorce and low self-esteem

Keep in mind the Ann Landers Law of Invitation:

"An adult should feel free to invite anyone he or she chooses to any kind of family affair or social event, regardless of who is talking to whom. It is then up to the invited person to accept or decline the invitation. If So-and-so says, 'I won't come if A, B, or C is invited,' the host or hostess should say, 'I'm so sorry. We will miss you.' Period."

often go hand-in-hand. But self-esteem can be improved. And luckily, weddings take time to plan, giving parents months to prepare facing the issues and people who intimidate them.

Have you ever watched someone get ready for a college reunion by losing weight, getting a new hairstyle, and buying a fabulous outfit? Weddings promote the same behavior. Parents can use the time to make new friends, cultivate interests, improve body image (weight, hairstyle, clothing, etc.), and learn new social skills. What a triumph to be able to greet a former spouse and the new family with confidence, charm, and grace.

The Guest List

The U.S. Census Bureau figures show that the rate of marriage continues to decline each decade. Nonetheless, it is estimated that an average of 200 people are invited to each of the 2.5 million weddings in the United States each year! Given the potential size of families, where parents are divorced and remarried, culling out names to get down to that number can be tough.

If the last divorce decree were to be issued today, the direct impact of divorce on weddings would continue for another twenty-five or thirty years. While the emotional fallout is well documented, the practical implications for family rituals are not.

It isn't exactly the way my generation of 1960s flower children envisioned togetherness, but the end result is similar to that concept of communal living. Multiple marriages and the proliferation of step relatives, along with the genealogical ones, are beginning to make all of us interrelated. And, we're all invited to important family rituals!

If you are planning a big wedding you have a lot more flexibility. You're able to think about friends and distant relatives, your parents' friends, business friends, and special people in your extracurricular activities.

You'll be getting names for the list from several people (you and your fiancé, your mothers, fathers, and stepparents), so sort names alphabetically to get one main list and pull out any duplicates. If your parents were divorced within the last few years, chances are that some names will show up more than once because they would have had many friends in common throughout their marriage.

If you need to know who has invited whom, use symbols as a code. For instance, bride's mother is (•) and bridegroom's father is (*). When the time comes to trim the list, these marks make it easier to make decisions fairly.

Wedding announcements, if you choose to send them, are mailed soon after the ceremony and are not sent to anyone receiving an invitation to the ceremony or reception. One trick in dealing with all these names is to put together your announcement list at the same time you compile the invitation list. Some names may fall into place without a struggle.

Group Symbolism

Always remember this when putting your list together: the objective of the wedding is to create a new family, not to destroy an old one!

Hurt feelings will result if you overlook a few people in a recognizable grouping while inviting others. And, it doesn't matter how far away they live. These may be family groups such as second cousins or great-aunts and great-uncles. In this case, the general idea is, "Invite a few, invite them all."

The key is relative numbers for groupings in your social family. Inviting your closest friend from the weekly bowling team or regular lunch group is one thing; inviting all but one or two people in the group is not nice.

The Final Tally

You will, no doubt, read about ways to survive the numbers crunch in wedding planning literature. When parents are divorced and remarried, the rule of thumb is to anticipate a slightly more complex situation.

Expanded families mean more people. However, most of the traditional cutting techniques will work for you, too.

For the reception immediately following the ceremony:

🐝 It's not socially necessary to invite dates for single guests unless they are in an obviously committed relationship—that is, engaged or living together.

🐝 Telephone to suggest that families may bring their children to the ceremony but that you must limit the number of reception guests. (This is a thoughtful way to make your position clear and might work if the events are held in separate locations.)

🐝 Cut your list by planning your ceremony and reception at a special location that's convenient for you but not necessarily convenient for all of your friends and relatives. Many people do travel to weddings in exciting locations and extend their visit to include a mini-vacation. However, they may think twice about a long trip without an added benefit.

🐝 You may also consider a small reception following the ceremony and celebrating your marriage with a larger group at a later date.

🐝 Entertain self-contained groupings of social friends at cocktail parties and mini-receptions several days or weeks before or after the wedding instead of inviting them to the reception on the day of the wedding ceremony.

🐝 Accept offers by close family members to host multiple receptions in their home towns. These various locations make it possible for long distance friends and relatives to attend.

🐝 Don't try to include these mini-receptions as part of the wedding by sending invitations along with the ceremony invitations or wedding announcements. These are formal or informal events to honor the newlyweds. They are not officially part of the main wedding event. These invitations follow normal protocol for reception and party entertaining that can be found in etiquette books.

🐝 You also have the opportunity to change your mind and elope. I'm not kidding. Couples who have made this decision insist that it's a great idea!

Nonetheless, before you throw in the towel on the wedding, it might help to know that, statistically, about 20 to 25 percent of guests who are invited to weddings will be unable to attend. If you send your invitations in time to get reasonably early "regrets," you may be able to invite people who have been on a waiting list.

Invitations

When a bride is young and her parents are not divorced, her parents assume responsibility for virtually the entire wedding. As sponsors and hosts of the ceremony and reception, their invitations reflect their traditional role as the bride's married parents.

Getting Out of Your Own Way

Your birth parents (or, if you were adopted, your adoptive parents) will always be your mother and father. That does not make it appropriate for you to coerce them into the awkward position of co-hosting ceremonies or parties when they are uncomfortable doing so. The idea is particularly absurd if either or both of your parents have remarried. Still, it is possible for the parents of the bride and groom to participate fully in the plans and events without being boxed into ill-fitting traditions. It's time to look at your relationship with each of your parents with a fresh approach.

If your divorced parents are like the majority who do not function smoothly in close proximity, you will need to come up with a way to accommodate their need to maintain some distance throughout the planning of the wedding. This can be gracefully accomplished by splitting the various components of the event between them or including other people who wish to be involved.

Remember the big picture. The wedding is made up of two parts:

> The Ceremony—Solemn recognition of a family, social, legal, religious ritual.

> The Reception—A party to celebrate completion of the ritual.

The ceremony is sponsored; the reception is hosted. The sponsor(s) may also be the host(s), as in intact families, but they may also be different! Since your parents are divorced they can each handle one of the two parts of the wedding, the ceremony or the reception. You will all need to decide who will be doing what before you order your invitations.

Dilemma of Style

Most decisions about what you put in writing on wedding invitations are based on common sense and simple courtesy. You want to say who, what, when, and where in a way that will reflect your values as well as your tastes.

What your invitations say and how they say it will give your guests clues about what to expect when they attend. For starters, guests will read about the date, time, and place of the ceremony and reception.

Most people on your invitation list probably know that your parents are divorced. So, they will also read between the lines and form an opinion about how smoothly your divorced parents are working together for the wedding, whether or not stepparents are actively included, and they'll even venture guesses about how the finances are being handled. These invitations are scrutinized for

The first glance at an invitation speaks volumes. Your choice of size, paper stock, plain or decorative borders, printing method, typeface, and phrasing all help recipients to visualize the wedding. You signal the formality and size of the gathering, what to wear, the ceremony sponsor(s) and the reception host(s) with whom the guest can discuss what gifts you'd like and, possibly, how to entertain you.

clues more carefully than those received for weddings without divorced parents.

A formal wedding invitation follows strict convention. Its rigid style frees you from the possibility of blunders. However, it's impossible to follow the "Mr. and Mrs." style (*Mr. and Mrs. Father and Mother*) when your parents are divorced. Since invitations can't be of the traditional variety, couples with divorced parents face confusion about whose–name–goes–where.

Unsolved Mysteries

Debates go on forever about who gets top billing on wedding invitations. Under the pressure of a deadline, more than one couple has made a snap decision. One bride I spoke with said that everyone was so concerned about whose–name–went–where that when the invitations arrived, she and her fiancé discovered that they'd left out the time of the wedding!

With counsel from etiquette books, printers, professional planners, and the parent with a checkbook, I've seen every imaginable example of style and wording. There are so many options, in fact, that it may look as if there's really no guidance at all. However, there is a logical and practical way to design your wedding invitations when your parents are divorced. Read on.

If you were adopted, your adoptive parents' role in your life is exactly the same as that of biological parents. For the sake of simplicity, in the following discussions, the terms "parents," "mother," and "father," cover both biological and adoptive mothers and fathers.

Certainly divorced parents can be sponsors of the ceremony if they have not disqualified themselves from this privilege by failing to honor their parenting responsibilities.

When your parents are divorced, the ceremony invitation is

usually issued by the parent with whom you lived, even if you are now living on your own. If this parent has remarried, the invitation is issued jointly with his or her spouse, your stepparent. The invitation announces their approval and blessing of your marriage.

In the past, wedding ceremony invitations were almost always issued by the bride's mother, either alone or with her new spouse. Even in cases where daughters live with their fathers, I have seen the families choose to have the bride's mother issue the ceremony invitation, just for the sake of convention.

Today, many brides have been parented by their stepmothers. If you have been living with your father and stepmother since early childhood, having little or no parenting contact with your mother, your mother is not really in a position to assume the role of mother-of-the-bride. This honor goes to your stepmother. Your mother is invited to attend the wedding as a guest.

Togetherness

Generally, the names of both divorced parents do not appear simultaneously on the ceremony invitation or on the combination ceremony and reception invitations. However, sometimes this rule begs to be broken. If you are in one of those rare situations where you and your divorced parents continue to function as one big happy family, you might opt to have both parents sponsor the ceremony.

Formal engravers are beginning to recognize divorced parents on the invitations and have a way of handling the situation. They "stack" the names. The preferred format is without the use of "and" between the names. The mother's name is listed first, with the bride's father (her ex-husband) on the next line.

The use of "and" in addressing envelopes indicates "married." For instance, Mr. Arthur Jones and Ms. Grace Straus, on the

Placement of names on the top of the ceremony invitation shows parental approval of the union. This honor of publicly blessing a child's marriage is earned by the parents who:

1. Take an active interest in your upbringing, studies, and everyday life.

2. Have standards to be enforced and values to be upheld.

3. Are available during sickness and difficult times and can be counted on for economic support.

4. Understand that simply loving you from a distance is not enough.

envelope, tells you that the couple is married and that Grace has retained her maiden name. Stacking the names, without the use of "and," indicates that the two people are not married to each other. It makes sense to keep that concept in the wording of invitations.

If the ceremony is not being sponsored by both parents, one parent issues the invitation and the other parent is an honored guest.

On the other hand, some cultures and religious groups traditionally have wedding invitations issued in the names of both sets of parents (bride's and bridegroom's) so it is not unheard of to include the entire parent group. The portfolio of examples later in this chapter includes a sample.

Who Hosts the Reception?

The hosts, whose cash and credit cards are paying for the reception party, are the ones to issue the reception invitations. A reception RSVP on the bottom of the ceremony invitation just doesn't work when the ceremony sponsors are not the same as the reception hosts. Traditional etiquette dictates separate ceremony and reception cards anyway . . . a convenience for divorced parents. Separate cards eliminate a lot of hassle and make it easier to plan the two functions separately right from the start.

The reception party host(s) will be one or any combination of the following:

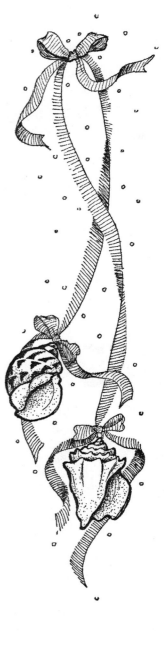

- ❦ Either one of your single parents.

- ❦ Either remarried parent (if remarried, you must include your stepparent's name—one's spouse is always considered a co-host for social events).

- ❦ Your fiancé's parents.

- ❦ You and your fiancé.

- ❦ Grandparents, brothers, sisters, or other relatives.

If there will be multiple hosts for the reception, you'll have to make a decision about name sequence. When discussing the topic with your various hosts, begin by suggesting alphabetical listing or financial contributions as a basis for the decision.

Those family members not hosting (planning and paying for) the reception party would be invited to attend as guests. They would not issue the invitation.

Respondez S'il Vous Plait

Whose return address should you use for the RSVP? Even things that seem so small can create confusion. The parent you choose must be able to handle:

- ❦ Tallying "accepts" and "regrets"

- ❦ Making suggestions for gift ideas (when asked)

- ❦ Telling guests where to mail wedding gifts (when asked)

- ❦ Passing along offers from friends and relatives to host pre- or post-wedding parties

Solo Performance

When families are not able to separate the wedding into the ceremony and the reception, or to sort out where financial contributions are and are not relevant, the bride and groom can issue the invitations in their own names.

Bride Alicia made this choice because, she said, "My father was paying for the wedding and didn't want my mother's name included on the invitation." Despite her father's wishes, Alicia didn't want to slight her mother so she and the groom issued the invitations. Another bride told me, "The wedding guests were invited by my fiancé and me in a formal invitation because I couldn't get my parents to agree on the wording."

The ceremony sponsor(s) and the reception host(s) can mail their invitations separately. However, two separate invitations may become confusing to guests when the wedding service and reception are held together.

You can resolve the confusion and expense of a duplicate mailing by enclosing the reception card in the same envelope with the ceremony card, even when the two are being issued by different family members. On the outer envelope, use the return address of the most organized host or sponsor. That person assumes the responsibility for matching names on the list with the

responses and keeping everyone informed on a regular basis.

It is nice to know who will be attending the ceremony but it is not essential. Head count is imperative for the reception where food and beverage plans are being made. This requires cooperation between sponsors and hosts. They don't have to love each other, however, to work together on this part of the project.

Brides usually use their own addresses for the RSVPs. Although this option is the most popular, it is not the most efficient. People don't always feel comfortable calling the bride to ask about gift ideas or other surprises. A better way to handle RSVPs is to leave the job of receiving them to the host of the reception.

Traditional Invitations

Begin with conventional wording to see what you like and what may be appropriate in your situation. Here are traditional ways of doing it:

- ❦ Phrasing for formal invitations is always in the third person (i.e., "their" versus "our").

- ❦ Invitations are engraved on traditional paper stock (ivory vellum, black ink, optional gold liner).

- ❦ Full names are used; abbreviations and initials are avoided.

- ❦ Titles Mr. and Mrs. precede names (Ms. is not used).

- ❦ "Honour" and "favour" are spelled with a "u."

- ❦ The phrase "request the honour of your presence" is used when the ceremony takes place in a house of worship.

- ❦ The phrase "request the pleasure of your company" is used when the ceremony takes place in a location other than a house of worship. (Separate reception cards also use this wording.)

- ❦ Include the wedding year on the invitation. (It is especially nice for keepsakes.)

- ❦ The bride's last name is used only when her last name differs from the sponsor(s) of the ceremony or host(s) of the reception. This situation occurs when the parents are divorced and the mother has remarried or when she has kept her maiden name in marriage.

- When guests are invited to both the ceremony and the reception, the larger invitation will be for the ceremony and the smaller card will be for the reception.

- When a small ceremony followed by a large reception is planned, the ceremony card will be small and the reception invitation will be larger.

- RSVPs. Response cards and envelopes are not considered in the best taste for formal invitations. Invitations carry an obligation to reply. (Nevertheless, you'll be sorry if you omit the stamped response card —a sad commentary on social manners these days.)

Non-Traditional Invitations

Guests who receive an alternative, lighthearted invitation understand that they're in for an unconventional time. Talk with local vendors or call the 800 numbers of wedding invitation printers advertised in all of the bridal magazines. Most are happy to provide you with catalogues and samples.

Alternatives to traditional formal invitations have a casual appearance. These invitations may:

- ❦ Exchange traditional third–person wording in favor of a more personal message.

- ❦ Be thermographed (raised letter printing that looks like engraving).

- ❦ Avoid the use of titles.

- ❦ Skip the "u" in "honour."

- ❦ Eliminate the year on the invitation.

- ❦ Use paper with floral or other designs.

- ❦ Be printed with ink in a shade that blends with your color scheme.

- ❦ Include web site, E–mail information.

It is also perfectly correct to use plain stationery and write out your own invitations for an informal wedding of fewer than fifty people.

In the portfolio of examples, I've used the mixed–and–matched names of my relatives for the various options in wording wedding invitations.

When designing invitations after their parent's divorce, brides most often ask for help about how to list their own name and their mother's name.

As a general rule, you will use your full name (first, middle, and last name) only if your last name differs from that of the ceremony sponsor(s) issuing the invitation.

Grace Louise

or

Grace Louise Straus

If your divorced mother has not remarried, the technically correct wording is for your mother to use her maiden name along with her married name.

Mrs. Cramer Straus

Another typical departure from strict convention is the popular use of Ms.

Ms. Margaret Cramer

or

Ms. Margaret Straus

or

Ms. Margaret Cramer Straus

When your mother has remarried and divorced again, she issues the invitations using her first name plus whatever last name she is currently using—her last married name or her maiden name.

Mrs. Margaret O'Brien

or

Ms. Margaret Cramer

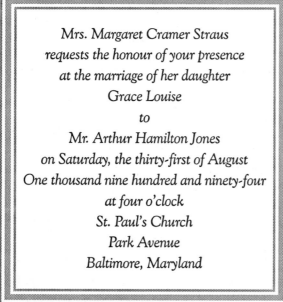

Mr. and Mrs. Louis Jacob Straus
request the honour of your presence
at the marriage of their daughter
Grace Louise
to
Mr. Arthur Hamilton Jones
on Saturday, the thirty-first of August
One thousand nine hundred and ninety-four
at four o'clock
St. Paul's Church
Park Avenue
Baltimore, Maryland

Mrs. Margaret Cramer Straus
requests the honour of your presence
at the marriage of her daughter
Grace Louise
to
Mr. Arthur Hamilton Jones
on Saturday, the thirty-first of August
One thousand nine hundred and ninety-four
at four o'clock
St. Paul's Church
Park Avenue
Baltimore, Maryland

Ceremony Invitations: A Portfolio of Examples

This portfolio will help you design the wording of your wedding invitation. Look for the bold heading that best describes your family circumstances and the parent(s) who will be your ceremony sponsor(s) and reception host(s).

Parents separated, but not legally divorced.

Option 1: The invitation is issued jointly in the traditional format.

Option 2: If the separated parents do not want to jointly issue the invitations, the parent with whom you make your home issues the ceremony invitations. (In past practice, even when the daughter lived in her father's home, the mother issued the invitations.) When your mother issues the ceremony invitations, she uses her formal married name. Note the use of "her daughter."

> Mrs. Margaret Cramer Straus
> Mr. Louis Jacob Straus
> request the honour of your presence
> at the marriage of their daughter
> Grace Louise
> to
> Mr. Arthur Hamilton Jones
> on Saturday, the thirty-first of August
> One thousand nine hundred and ninety-four
> at four o'clock
> St. Paul's Church
> Park Avenue
> Baltimore, Maryland

> Mrs. Margaret Cramer Straus
> requests the honour of your presence
> at the marriage of her daughter
> Grace Louise
> to
> Mr. Arthur Hamilton Jones
> on Saturday, the thirty-first of August
> One thousand nine hundred and ninety-four
> at four o'clock
> St. Paul's Church
> Park Avenue
> Baltimore, Maryland

Parents, divorced but "friendly," issue the ceremony invitation jointly.

Both names may be listed on the invitation. The preferred format is to stack the names, mother's name first, without using the word "and." The form "their daughter" is used.

Mother, not remarried, issues the ceremony invitations.

The socially correct and formal wording is for your mother to use Mrs. and her maiden name along with her last name (Mrs. Cramer Straus).

Today, women are more comfortable with one of these other appropriate choices:

Mrs. Margaret Cramer

or

Mrs. Margaret Cramer Straus

or

Ms. Margaret Straus

Mother, remarried, issues the ceremony invitation with your father.

Your divorced parents have a friendly relationship and want to sponsor your wedding together. This invitation used "their daughter" and the bride's last name because it is different from one of her sponsors.

Mrs. Richard Burr O'Brien
Mr. Louis Jacob Straus
request the honour of your presence
at the marriage of their daughter
Grace Louise Straus
to
Mr. Arthur Hamilton Jones
on Saturday, the thirty-first of August
One thousand nine hundred and ninety-four
at four o'clock
St. Paul's Church
Park Avenue
Baltimore, Maryland

Mother, remarried, issues the ceremony invitation without stepfather.

A married parent usually issues invitations jointly with his/her spouse. If there are extenuating circumstances, your mother could send the ceremony invitations alone using her new married name. Note the use of "her daughter" and the inclusion of the bride's last name because it is different from the sponsor's.

Mrs. Richard Burr O'Brien
requests the honour of your presence
at the marriage of her daughter
Grace Louise Straus
to
Mr. Arthur Hamilton Jones
on Saturday, the thirty-first of August
One thousand nine hundred and ninety-four
at four o'clock
St. Paul's Church
Park Avenue
Baltimore, Maryland

Mother, remarried, issues the ceremony invitation with stepfather.

You have lived with your mother and stepfather and have little or no parenting contact with your father or are very close to your stepfather.

You have three options. In each one, the bride's full name is used because it is different from the sponsors. You can choose:

her daughter

or

Mrs. O'Brien's daughter

or

their daughter

Mr. and Mrs. Richard Burr O'Brien
request the honour of your presence
at the marriage of her daughter
Grace Louise Straus
to
Mr. Arthur Hamilton Jones
on Saturday, the thirty-first of August
One thousand nine hundred and ninety-four
at four o'clock
St. Paul's Church
Park Avenue
Baltimore, Maryland

Mr. and Mrs. Richard Burr O'Brien
request the honour of your presence
at the marriage of their daughter
Grace Louise Straus
to
Mr. Arthur Hamilton Jones
on Saturday, the thirty-first of August
One thousand nine hundred and ninety-four
at four o'clock
St. Paul's Church
Park Avenue
Baltimore, Maryland

Mr. and Mrs. Richard Burr O'Brien
request the honour of your presence
at the marriage of Mrs.O'Brien's daughter
Grace Louise Straus
to
Mr. Arthur Hamilton Jones
on Saturday, the thirty-first of August
One thousand nine hundred and ninety-four
at four o'clock
St. Paul's Church
Park Avenue
Baltimore, Maryland

> Mr. and Mrs. Richard Burr O'Brien
> Mr. Louis Jacob Straus
> request the honour of your presence
> at the marriage of their daughter
> Grace Louise Straus
> to
> Mr. Arthur Hamilton Jones
> on Saturday, the thirty-first of August
> One thousand nine hundred and ninety-four
> at four o'clock
> St. Paul's Church
> Park Avenue
> Baltimore, Maryland

Mother remarried, father not remarried. The ceremony invitation is issued jointly.

Twenty plus years ago, a distinguished stationery company refused to print an invitation with this combination of names because it wasn't "proper." This was the first of eight children's weddings. The printer has lost a lot of business over the years. (Just for fun, I contacted this stationery company. Their position has not changed!) Note the use of "their daughter" and the bride's last name.

> Mr. Louis Jacob Straus
> requests the honour of your presence
> at the marriage of his daughter
> Grace Louise
> to
> Mr. Arthur Hamilton Jones
> on Saturday, the thirty-first of August
> One thousand nine hundred and ninety-four
> at four o'clock
> St. Paul's Church
> Park Avenue
> Baltimore, Maryland

Father, not remarried, issues the ceremony invitation.

You have made your home with your father and have little or no contact with your mother. Use "his daughter." Do not use your last name because it is the same as your sponsor's.

Father, remarried, issues the ceremony invitation with stepmother.

You have lived with your father and stepmother and have little or no contact with your mother or are very close to your stepmother. Your last name is not used because it is the same as your sponsor's. You will choose:

his daughter

or

Mr. Straus' daughter

or

their daughter

Mr. and Mrs. Louis Jacob Straus
request the honour of your presence
at the marriage of his daughter
Grace Louise
to
Mr. Arthur Hamilton Jones
on Saturday, the thirty-first of August
One thousand nine hundred and ninety-four
at four o'clock
St. Paul's Church
Park Avenue
Baltimore, Maryland

Mr. and Mrs. Louis Jacob Straus
request the honour of your presence
at the marriage of their daughter
Grace Louise
to
Mr. Arthur Hamilton Jones
on Saturday, the thirty-first of August
One thousand nine hundred and ninety-four
at four o'clock
St. Paul's Church
Park Avenue
Baltimore, Maryland

Mr. and Mrs. Louis Jacob Straus
request the honour of your presence
at the marriage of Mr. Straus' daughter
Grace Louise
to
Mr. Arthur Hamilton Jones
on Saturday, the thirty-first of August
One thousand nine hundred and ninety-four
at four o'clock
St. Paul's Church
Park Avenue
Baltimore, Maryland

> Ms. Margaret Straus O'Brien
> and
> Mr. and Mrs. Louis Jacob Straus
> request the honour of your presence
> at the marriage of their daughter
> Grace Louise
> to
> Mr. Arthur Hamilton Jones
> on Saturday, the thirty-first of August
> One thousand nine hundred and ninety-four
> at four o'clock
> St. Paul's Church
> Park Avenue
> Baltimore, Maryland

Father remarried, mother not remarried. The ceremony invitation issued jointly.

Bride's last name is not used because her name is the same as her parent's. Mother may choose the format of her name from the list on page 71. Note the use of "their daughter."

> Mrs. Richard Burr O'Brien
> Mr. Lou Jacob Straus
> request the honour of your presence
> at the marriage of their daughter
> Grace Louise Straus
> to
> Mr. Arthur Hamilton Jones
> on Saturday, the thirty-first of August
> One thousand nine hundred and ninety-four
> at four o'clock
> St. Paul's Church
> Park Avenue
> Baltimore, Maryland

Mother and father remarried, jointly issue the ceremony invitation.

Parents who have both maintained a close relationship with their daughter sometimes co-sponsor the ceremony without their new spouses. (Remember that sponsoring the ceremony is giving approval to the marriage. Hosting the reception means paying for the party.) The bride's last name is used because it is not the same as one of her sponsors. Note the use of "their" daughter.

Mother and father remarried. Parents and stepparents jointly issue the ceremony invitation.

When relations are friendly and both couples have honored their parenting commitment, all four names may be listed as sponsors of the ceremony.

Names are "stacked" with mother and stepfather on the first line, father and stepmother on the second line. Use "their daughter." The bride's last name is used because it differs from one of the sponsors.

> Mr. and Mrs. Richard Burr O'Brien
> Mr. and Mrs. Louis Jacob Straus
> request the honour of your presence
> at the marriage of their daughter
> Grace Louise Straus
> to
> Mr. Arthur Hamilton Jones
> on Saturday, the thirty-first of August
> One thousand nine hundred and ninety-four
> at four o'clock
> St. Paul's Church
> Park Avenue
> Baltimore, Maryland

Groom's parents issue the ceremony invitation.

It is unusual for the bridegroom's parents to issue the ceremony invitations. It may be the choice in cases where the bride's parents are deceased or do not wish to participate or give their blessing. When the groom's parents have a particularly close relationship with the bride, this invitation indicates their approval. Use the title "Miss" and the bride's last name. Note the use of "to their son."

> Mr. and Mrs. Malcolm Conrad Jones
> request the honour of your presence
> at the marriage of
> Miss Grace Louise Straus
> to their son
> Mr. Arthur Hamilton Jones
> on Saturday, the thirty-first of August
> One thousand nine hundred and ninety-four
> at four o'clock
> St. Paul's Church
> Park Avenue
> Baltimore, Maryland

Every parent the bride has ever had jointly issues the ceremony invitation.

I've seen families where friendship and parenting commitments survived the rigors of divorces and remarriages. There could be lots of different combinations. This example will give you a visual idea of how it would look if the sponsors were an unmarried mother (twice divorced), father and stepmother, former stepfather and his new wife. Note the use of "their daughter" and the bride's last name to show whose daughter she is.

Bride's and groom's parents issue the ceremony invitation.

It is becoming popular to include the groom's parents' names on the ceremony invitation. In some cultures, this is a tradition. In the United States, this is done to acknowledge a significant financial contribution to the wedding. In this invitation, both the bride's and the groom's parents are divorced and remarried.

If, in reality, both sets of parents are co–hosting (paying for) the reception party, it would be more appropriate to list them on the reception invitation. See the sample in the portfolio examples under "Reception Invitations."

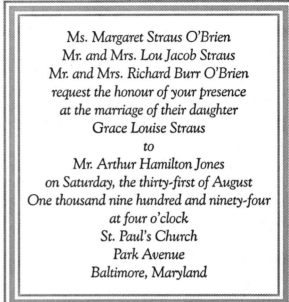

Ms. Margaret Straus O'Brien
Mr. and Mrs. Lou Jacob Straus
Mr. and Mrs. Richard Burr O'Brien
request the honour of your presence
at the marriage of their daughter
Grace Louise Straus
to
Mr. Arthur Hamilton Jones
on Saturday, the thirty-first of August
One thousand nine hundred and ninety-four
at four o'clock
St. Paul's Church
Park Avenue
Baltimore, Maryland

Mr. and Mrs. Richard Burr O'Brien
Mr. and Mrs. Lou Jacob Straus
Mr. and Mrs. Joseph Paul Rizzo
Mr. and Mrs. Malcolm Conrad Jones
request the honour of your presence
at the marriage of
Grace Louise Straus
and
Arthur Hamilton Jones
on Saturday, the thirty-first of August
One thousand nine hundred and ninety-four
at four o'clock
St. Paul's Church
Park Avenue
Baltimore, Maryland

Mrs. Lou Jacob Straus
requests the honour of your presence
at the marriage of her stepdaughter
Grace Louise
to
Mr. Arthur Hamilton Jones
on Saturday, the thirty-first of August
One thousand nine hundred and ninety-four
at four o'clock
St. Paul's Church
Park Avenue
Baltimore, Maryland

Stepmother issues the ceremony invitation for her stepdaughter.

This situation can occur when both of your parents are deceased. The term "stepdaughter" is used, whether or not your stepmother has remarried. If she has remarried, your full name is used because you do not have the same last name.

Bride and groom issue the ceremony invitations.

When there is not a clear or obvious choice, the bride and groom can issue their own invitations. These invitations may look formal due to the choices of paper stock and engraving. More often, however, they have a casual appearance with the use of floral or other designs, and shades of ink that blend with the wedding color scheme. Some couples create their own invitations using a computer.

Bride and groom issue the ceremony invitations, names listed at top.

This option produces the widest variation on wording for wedding invitations. Invitations often use the formal layout, without titles. Other options are:

Miss Grace Louise Straus

and

Mr. Arthur Hamilton Jones

or

Ms. Grace Louise Straus

and

Mr. Arthur Hamilton Jones

Grace Louise Straus
and
Arthur Hamilton Jones
request the honour of your presence
at their marriage
on Saturday, the thirty-first of August
One thousand nine hundred and ninety-four
at four o'clock
St. Paul's Church
Park Avenue
Baltimore, Maryland

Bride and groom issue the ceremony invitations, names listed in the middle.

Another option is to place the "request" before the names. The invitation in this example does not use titles. Other choices are:

Ms. (or Miss) Grace Straus

to

Mr. Arthur Jones

or

Ms. (or Miss) Grace Louise Straus

to

Mr. Arthur Hamilton Jones

Other wording to replace "request the honour of your presence."

*invite you to a celebration
where they will share marriage vows*

*invite you to share in their joy
of the beginning of their new life together
when they exchange marriage vows*

*invite you to share in their joy
when they exchange marriage vows
and begin their new life together*

*invite you to share in the ceremony
uniting them in marriage*

*request the honour of your presence
at their marriage ceremony*

*have chosen the first day
of their new life together*

*The honour of your presence
is requested at the marriage of
Grace Louise Straus
and
Arthur Hamilton Jones
on Saturday, the thirty-first of August
One thousand nine hundred and ninety-four
at four o'clock
St. Paul's Church
Park Avenue
Baltimore, Maryland*

In the following examples, notice the change from the formal third-person phrasing to the less formal first-person phrasing:

*joyously invite you to witness the uniting
of our lives into one*

*invite you to share with us
the joy of our marriage*

*invite you to share in the ceremony
uniting us in marriage*

*invite you to be with us
as we begin our new life together*

Bride and groom issue the ceremony invitation, names listed at the bottom.

Another option gives all of the wedding information first and places the bride's and groom's names at the bottom. This format allows for a great variety of different wordings. Variations may use titles and omit middle names.

We invite you to be with us
as we begin our new life together
on Saturday, the thirty-first of August
nineteen hundred and ninety-four
at four o'clock in the afternoon
St. Paul's Church
Park Avenue
Baltimore, Maryland
Grace Louise Straus
and
Arthur Hamilton Jones

Together with their parents
Grace Louise Straus
and
Arthur Hamilton Jones
invite you to share with them
a celebration of love
The ceremony will be
on Saturday, the thirty-first of August
One thousand nine hundred and ninety-four
at four o'clock
St. Paul's Church
Park Avenue
Baltimore, Maryland

Bride and groom issue the ceremony invitation, acknowledge parents.

"Together with their parents," "along with their families," "Together with our parents," and "and our parents," are very popular combinations. Sometimes these words come before the names of the bride and groom, as shown in this invitation.

You can also put the names first:

Grace Louise Straus
and
Arthur Hamilton Jones
together with their parents
or
and our parents

Reception Invitations: A Portfolio of Examples

The size of your reception card will be determined by the information it must contain. Sizes range from the traditional small enclosure to a card that may be almost the size of your ceremony invitation.

Sponsor(s) of the ceremony are the same as the host(s) for the reception party.

The reception cards do not need to repeat the names so the cards may be the standard smaller card.

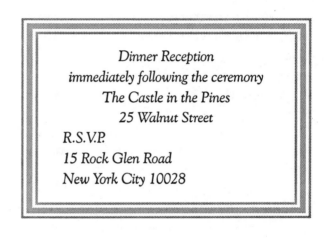

Dinner Reception
immediately following the ceremony
The Castle in the Pines
25 Walnut Street
R.S.V.P.
15 Rock Glen Road
New York City 10028

The ceremony sponsors and reception hosts are different; the reception invitation issued by the host(s) of the party.

It is common for the bride's divorced parents to issue the ceremony invitation together (see page 76). One of her parents with his or her new spouse may issue the reception invitation. For instance, if your mother and father sponsor the ceremony and your father and stepmother host the reception, your reception card will look like the example and will be larger than usual to accommodate more information.

Mr. and Mrs. Louis Jacob Straus
request the pleasure of your company
at the marriage reception of his daughter
Grace Louise
and
Arthur Hamilton Jones
immediately following the ceremony
The Castle in the Pines
Baltimore

Reply card enclosed

The most popular choice.

When your parents have been remarried for many years and you lived with your mother and stepfather, your mother and stepfather issue the ceremony invitation. Your father and stepmother (who often pay the lion's share of the party expenses) issue the reception invitation.

When the groom's family shares in the planning and expenses of the reception, to be socially correct, their names are included as hosts on the reception invitation.

In this example, the reception hosts are the bride's two sets of parents jointly with the groom's father and stepmother.

> Mr. and Mrs. Richard Burr O'Brien
> Mr. and Mrs. Louis Jacob Straus
> Mr. and Mrs. Malcolm Conrad Jones
> request the pleasure of your company
> at the marriage reception of
> Grace Louise Straus
> and
> Arthur Hamilton Jones
> immediately following the ceremony
> The Castle in the Pines

Decisions, Decisions, Decisions

If you are thoroughly confused, take a break. When you come back and are ready to tackle the wording of the invitations, consider working backwards. Decide whether you want a formal or informal "feel" and you will already have some decisions made for you. For instance, formal is using full names with titles; casual is using first and last names without titles. What about placement of names, phrasing the verse, and the when/where details?

If you have the format laid out, it may be easier to talk about which names to insert. If you go strictly formal, only your mother and father issue the ceremony invitations. When you acknowledge practical reality such as the emotionally supportive parent with whom you made your home and the parent who is footing the bills, it may be easier to give each of your parents a "logical," rather than traditional, placement on the ceremony and the reception invitations.

Your layout talents are faced with a challenge! Just remember that in the end, you'll become newlyweds—no matter how the invitations are worded.

Success in marriage does not come merely through finding the right mate, but through being the right mate.

— Barnett Brickner

Setting the Scene

If a mother's biggest concern is that a stepmother will try to upstage her, a bride's most overwhelming wedding worry may be how to choose her escort for walking down the aisle.

Traditionally, fathers have been awarded this privilege automatically. When divorced fathers and their daughters have maintained a good, reciprocal relationship, brides comfortably follow tradition.

All too often, however, divorced fathers and their daughters have not maintained loving, positive relationships. The need to select an aisle escort forces these brides to acknowledge that their fathers do not fit their idealized image, and they often experience a great deal of ambivalence about asking their fathers to escort them to the altar.

One bride described the dilemma clearly, "Do I have a duty to 'honor thy father' at my wedding if, for years, he chose not to 'honor thy daughter?'" Another bride put the problem a different way, "I'm pretty sure that my dad loves me but his behavior hasn't been very responsible."

Occasionally, a bride of divorced parents fits into her mother's wedding dress and loves the idea of wearing it for her own wedding. If this is your situation and you don't feel that it would be "unlucky," the idea has a nice sentimental touch.

Stepmothers always appreciate information on appropriate dress. If either you or your fiancé has a stepmother who will be attending the wedding, it is thoughtful to pass along information about what your mother and the groom's mother are wearing. As one bride put it, "I didn't want her to be embarrassed by wearing a dress that was too similar to my mother's dress." Sharing the information will also give her a guideline as to style and length of dress that will blend in appropriately.

In assessing your own situation, you'll probably find yourself sidetracked from the wedding plans while you come to grips with this relationship. If you and your father had a falling-out years ago, it may be hard to admit that you don't want to ask your father to escort you—and even harder to face the consequences of your decision.

Some brides don't give up on their fathers even when they've been abandoned without a backward glance. They don't want to feel guilty about worsening the poor relationship or publicly exposing it. They hope that their act of love and kindness will change their father's behavior. This raises a philosophical question. Do you consider the role of escort your father's natural right or an honor bestowed for being a moral, protective, and concerned parent?

A word of advice from those who have gone before you. "Whatever decision you make, meet privately with your father and tell him in advance." When parents are divorced, it is not uncommon or unreasonable for a bride to offer this honor to someone other than her father. If this is your intention, it is thoughtful to tell him. That way, your father will not have false expectations or hear about your plans from someone else.

Fathers

As it turns out, there are many options for getting the bride down the aisle. If you want a dad to escort you down the aisle, you actually have three choices: father, stepfather, or both of them

If a bride's father is alive, the chances are likely that he will be the choice. Whenever humanly possible, brides typically pick their fathers for the aisle walk. Even daughters who were very young at the time of their parents' divorce clearly see a distinction between fathers and stepfathers when they grow older. Although there may be emotional ties to both, there are, in addition, strong biological ties to just one. This bond of blood relation often leads brides to ask their fathers as an affirmation of lineage.

On the other hand, some daughters prefer their stepfathers because they think of them as more loving and more reliable than their fathers. When brides have been reared by mothers and stepfathers and had little or no contact with their fathers, the stepfather may be clearly the appropriate choice. In this event, the stepfather functions as the bride's parent throughout the wedding, just as he did while she was growing up.

Bride Barbara regarded her father as an outsider. Although he never missed a visitation day, supported her financially, and loved her very much, she had never gotten over a very nasty custody trial. In addition, she had lived with her stepfather since she was in preschool. When she became engaged, there was no discussion —her stepfather would walk her down the aisle.

An increasingly popular third alternative exists when you have a father and a stepfather who both deserve the honor. You can have the two of them walk you down the aisle. If you like this idea, check to make sure that the aisle you've chosen is wide enough for three people—especially if one of them will be wearing a very full skirt!

Stepfathers dress as the other guests do, or, if they are participating in the ceremony, they dress in an outfit similar to the other men in the wedding party.

One bride told me, "My father is my father but my stepfather is my parent." A valid distinction: A father is a biological happenstance; a parent nurtures the child.

Another bride solved her dilemma by asking both fathers to walk with her; "a dad on each arm."

Having divorced parents results in many other variations on this part of the ceremony. Fathers are not the only possible alternatives for your aisle escort.

Brothers, uncles, grandfathers, and godfathers are popular choices when you want to stick with the tradition of your escort being a male member of your family.

Shawna describes her big day. "My mom and dad walked me halfway down the aisle. Then, my dad sat down and my mom gave me away, which was symbolic of our lives."

In this time of single-parent families, many brides are reared by their mothers. As a result, an increasing number of brides are asking their mothers to escort them down the aisle. Bride Diana's mother admitted, "I hadn't seen it done before but I was flattered when my daughter asked me to accompany her." If you are particularly close to your mother, this may be an appropriate solution.

The Dramatic Entrance

Some bridal couples find that conventional choices are impossible for their families. They start from scratch and brainstorm ideas.

Brides and bridegrooms may decide to walk down the aisle together. This choice usually means walking the entire length of the aisle together. A variation is for your groom to meet you at the halfway point. You start down the aisle from the back and your groom begins his walk from the front—you meet halfway and proceed together to where the officiant is standing.

Incorporating traditions from many cultures may also provide a viable alternative. For instance, Jewish tradition involves the entire family by having them all walk down the aisle with the bridal couple. The families remain standing together throughout the ceremony.

Of course, there is always the solo entrance. Typical of her pragmatic independence, bride Marilyn said proudly, "I walked down the aisle by myself!"

Jim, a pleased father, described his family's solution as a combination of traditional and non-traditional. "I walked my daughter down the aisle. At the foot of the altar, all other parents and stepparents joined us. When the minister asked, 'Who gives this woman in marriage?' the answer, 'We do,' came from all of us."

Through the years, it has become a tradition to invite sisters and brothers to be in the wedding party. In today's complex families, this honor also goes to extended family members. The greatest compliment you can pay a step or half sibling is to invite him or her to be in your wedding. The gesture has brought many families together.

"My half sister was our flower girl," Joseph told me.

"My stepmother and father had been married for 10 years. I asked my stepmother to do readings as part of our Catholic service so she could be part of the ceremony," John noted.

"We arranged for everyone, steps and 'regular' couples, to be written into the wine ceremony at the altar," Hollie explained.

Floral Arrangements & Wedding Attire

Florists function as decorating consultants for arrangements that suit the tone of the occasion, whether formal or casual. Most of your flower decisions are discussed in traditional wedding planning books. In addition to decorating the ceremony and reception sites, flowers may adorn special people.

If your extended family is large, a number of mothers and grandmothers, fathers, grandfathers and step relatives may expect to be distinguished with corsages and boutonnières. Of course, you and your fiancé and your attendants are appropriately adorned. The most popular way of dealing with the cast of thousands has been to include everyone in the family with color-coordinated flowers.

Hearts and Flowers

Personal flowers are a small but significant gesture of affection and respect. Brides and bridegrooms especially enjoy giving them to stepfamily members as a way of saying, "I'm glad you're part of my family, particularly on this special day." Bride Mimi was very clear about her objectives. She said, "I wanted to set our families apart, literally and figuratively, from the other guests."

If you want to give flowers, it is important to coordinate style and colors with both the wedding theme and the personal preferences of the recipients. In addition to mothers, it might also be appropriate to provide a small corsage to friends and extended family members who perform special services, such as attending the guest book.

A woman may wear her corsage at her shoulder, on a handbag, or on her wrist. The key men, namely the groom and each of the bride's and groom's fathers, usually have boutonnières similar to, but a bit larger than, the rest of the men in the wedding party.

Petal Dropping

Florists tell me that it helps to know about family relationships that depart from the "norm." For instance, if you have two mothers (your mother and stepmother) attending, the corsages may be quite similar. One florist explains how she handles delicate family relationships: "I am very careful not to put 'Mom' on both boxes. I put 'Mom' on one box and the first name of the stepmother on the other box."

Ask a friend to personally take delivery of the corsages and boutonnières. This person will be responsible for distributing them and pinning them on the recipients. This can eliminate worries for you, especially if a lot of people are receiving flowers.

Change of Heart

Some couples decide not to provide corsages for any of the mothers or grandmothers for a very practical reason—flowers can ruin the look of an expensive dress. This is a topic for discussion among all the women because the final decision should be a uniform "all or nothing."

One compromise: There is something to be said in favor of providing a single, small flower. For instance, a rosebud will identify family members to guests and to the photographer.

Beverly says,

One non-traditional bride asked her stepbrothers and half brothers(four in all) to be her attendants. For this outdoor wedding they wore light-colored shirts and slacks and a rose boutonnière. Each had a small piece to say in the ceremony leading up to lighting a unity candle.

Flowers and Their Meanings

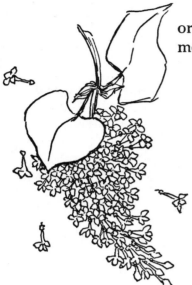

All of the most popular flowers are associated with some noble or desirable quality. The list below includes some favorite and more unusual flowers and their special meanings:

Apple blossoms—good fortune

Carnation—distinction

Chrysanthemum—friendship

Daffodil—joy

Daisy—loyalty

Forget-Me-Not—true love

Gardenia—joy

Heather—admiration

Lilac—first emotions of love

Lily of the Valley—return of happiness

Iris—wisdom

Ivy—friendship

Magnolia—nobility

Myrtle—love

Orange Blossom—loveliness

Orchid—beauty

Pansy—you occupy my thoughts

Peony—happiness

Rose—deep love

Stephanotis—happiness in marriage

Sweetpeas—delicate pleasures

Zinnia—goodness

Ceremony Seating

The aerial view of wedding ceremony seating is the same for weddings with or without a divorce in the family. These arrangements are taken for granted when the usher asks, "Are you on the bride's side or the groom's?" Only a ceremony novice is surprised.

An amused usher told me this story: "While I was walking a father and his young son to their seats, the little boy asked his dad, in a loud whisper, "Are we taking sides already?"

"In the Ribbons"

Contrary to popular opinion, the aisles are not roped off so your groom can't get away. The first four to six rows of the chairs or pews are usually sectioned off for family members. If someone ties the ribbons into knots instead of lovely white bows, you'll know to watch for turmoil!

As a general rule, the first row of "In the Ribbons" honored seating is reserved for the bridesmaids and ushers, if needed. The second row is for parents, stepparents, grandparents and possibly siblings, including step siblings and and half siblings. The next rows are reserved for aunts, uncles, and their families and special friends.

For a Christian wedding ceremony, the left side (as you face the altar and officiant) is for the bride's family and friends, the right side is for the groom's family and friends. In Reform and Conservative Jewish weddings, it is the reverse. Men and women are often segregated for Orthodox Jewish services.

Wedding ceremonies usually take place in the bride's territory. That may present challenges to family members and guests who have to travel a distance. There's always the possibility of these travelers getting lost and trailing in late.

Typical ways of letting your ushers know who sits in honored seating are to:

❧ Provide your honored guests with pew cards or "In the Ribbons" cards (enclose with the invitations). The small card will look similar to the one below.

The number of the pew is written in by hand.

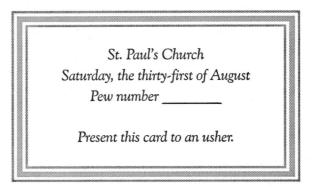

> *St. Paul's Church*
> *Saturday, the thirty-first of August*
> *Pew number* _____
>
> *Present this card to an usher.*

❧ Provide your ushers with the list of appropriate names.

Seating Etiquette

Rules of etiquette are created so people can feel more secure in social situations. Even though divorce has been around for a long time, a lot of the wedding etiquette rules still need to be molded, or cut, to fit the situation. Here are some seating guidelines.

Parents who sponsor the ceremony sit together in the second row of the "In the Ribbons" seats—if they are not divorced. Only on very rare occasions do divorced parents sit next to each other in the second row. Divorced parents, who have not remarried, are the most likely to sit in the same row, often with relatives seated between them.

However, even if your parents are comfortable with the idea, it is not practical for all parents and stepparents and their companions to sit together in the second row of seats. If your father walks you down the aisle, he'll need to slip unobtrusively into the aisle seat when his escort duties are completed. With his wife or date to his left, that places your mother third in the row where her view of the bridal procession may be obstructed. If your mother's husband or date needs to sit as a buffer between the two women, your mother is now fourth in the row and even farther away from "the action." The logistics simply don't work.

I've also heard of remarried biological parents electing to sit together in the first parent row, along with other children of that marriage. At one such ceremony, stepparents and the children from the new marriages sat in the rows directly behind them. This arrangement is seldom chosen because it ignores basic "couples etiquette."

Since many out-of-town guests may be known to your groom's parents, his parents might have an important role to play prior to the ceremony. A graceful way to be sure that all attendees receive a warm welcome is to have the groom's parents do the honors. They can take up stations near the entrance a little early in order to welcome guests as they arrive for the ceremony. In addition to being practical—so guests know they have arrived at the right wedding—I think it's a lovely social gesture. The groom's parents have the honor of being the initial greeters!

Your Mother's Seat

When your parents are divorced and they choose not to sit together, your mother almost always gets to sit in the second row. She also gets to select her seatmates.

Mothers frequently share this row of honor with their other children and their parents. If your mother is remarried, her spouse (your stepfather) joins her in the second row. If she is single, her significant other usually sits there too. A casual escort is seated with the other guests.

Your stepmother is seated in the second row as mother-of-the-bride when she, and not your mother, reared you. In these cases, if your mother is present, she and her husband (your stepfather) are most often seated as honored guests "In the Ribbons." If that feels uncomfortable for any reason, you may decide to stick to convention and keep your mother's place in the second row.

This seating format also applies to your groom's mother(s) on the other side of the aisle.

On the day of the wedding, the last person escorted to a seat by the usher is the mother-of-the-bride who is given the honor of sitting in the second row. Her entrance signals the beginning of the ceremony.

Your Father's Seat

When your divorced parents do not choose to sit together, your father claims the third row. If tension is palpable between your mother and father, he may leave a buffer row and move back to the fourth row from the front. He too gets to choose his seatmates.

A single father shares his row of honor with his parents and siblings. Sometimes children who are not in the wedding party will split up so that both parents are seated with at least one of their offspring.

If your father is remarried, his spouse (your stepmother) joins him in his designated third or fourth row. If he is single, he invites his significant other to be seated with him. A casual escort is seated with the other guests.

The Hot Seat

Stepparents sit with their spouses for the ceremony. In families that simply refuse to get along for a few hours, stepparents may choose to be seated with the other guests. In extreme cases, some stepparents do not attend the ceremony at all.

Bridal couples tell me that the seating of stepparents is a big topic of discussion. Mothers and fathers frequently harbor strong resentments toward each other's new spouses. Nonetheless, according to most reports, this seating issue gets ironed out as part of an overall family philosophy toward the wedding. Various family members are consistently either "In" or "Out" of the planning and festivities so the pieces may fall into place naturally.

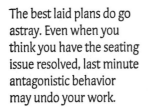

The best laid plans do go astray. Even when you think you have the seating issue resolved, last minute antagonistic behavior may undo your work.

A family member reported this story: "My cousin Dorrien has been married for 15 years to a man with five children. She has a warm relationship with her stepdaughter, the bride, but she has problems with her stepson, the bride's brother, who was an usher. Instead of being seated in the designated place, the stepson escorted her to the very last pew of the church." Certainly the bride had not intended for her stepmother to be treated so inconsiderately.

Surprise!

Uninvited guests have been known to show up for the ceremony. Ann, a startled bride, told me, "When my ex-husband and former mother-in-law joined the other guests, I wasn't sure what to do. They sat unobtrusively in the back of the church so I simply greeted them as I did all of the other guests."

If you have reason to anticipate trouble, discuss this with your ushers so that they may be prepared. Any potential for serious problems should be discussed with security personnel.

Jan, a wedding consultant, told about one wedding where the father of the bride came in late, sat in the last row of the church, and left as soon as the couple said their vows. "He said nothing and left before anyone could even greet him."

You may have more well-wishers than you realize.

In our life there is
a single color,
as on an artist's palette, which
provides the meaning
of life and art.
It is the color of love.
— Marc Chagall

Photographing the Wedding

When there has been a divorce in the family, virtually every bridal couple has definite ideas about the kind of family photographs they want taken. The best way to think about it is to visualize what you will see in your wedding album (or video) five or ten years from now. Choices range from a portfolio of formal posed portraits, primarily of the wedding party, to mostly candid pictures including everybody. You must decide which format you want your photographer to emphasize.

The Big Day

Good wedding photography captures the expressions and life of the moment, regardless of the style you choose. Photographers say that it's best to avoid interrupting the festivities by taking up huge blocks of time for formal pictures. Arrange for a few formal portraits to be taken quickly so you can join your guests at the reception party.

Weddings chock full of divorced parents usually require special sensitivity and tact. When you are interviewing a photographer, ask if he or she has photographed weddings with divorced parents in attendance. Another clue to a good match may be a photographer who has witnessed a divorce in his own family. It might provide the photographer with a heightened awareness of photo situations that you or your family members may find uncomfortable. Sometimes, former spouses are adamant that they don't want to be photographed together under any circumstances.

In addition to technical skills with a camera, you need a photographer who has "people skills."

Be sure to identify the key people for your photographer. You or a helper can point them out as they arrive at the reception.

Experienced wedding photographers stress that it is important to let them know about the subtleties of family relationships in advance. Obviously, photographers like to be saved from unnecessary embarrassment at the wedding—their own or your guests' discomfort. An awkward scene over attempts to memorialize former couples in pictures can spoil the festive atmosphere.

You can also ask the photographer to stay nearby while you greet guests at the entrance. Another key-person signal is corsages and boutonnières.

However, wedding photographers often caution their clients: "Don't overplan my duties." Good photographers have a sixth sense about important pictures, including all of the traditional ones such as multiple generations and various parent combinations. They also know that you'll seat categories of people together, such as college classmates or colleagues from work. These group pictures are taken during the routine course of the reception.

"Correct" or "Incorrect"

Depending upon whom you ask and what you read, divorced parents *should* or *should not* appear in the same formal wedding photographs. The best advice is, "Ask your mother and father how they feel about the pictures."

Some divorced parents are friendly enough to step into the same pictures; others are not. This is a sensitive boundary issue for many parents and stepparents. As a matter of fact, it's a good idea to ask all of your parents how they feel about picture taking.

On the other hand, sometimes there's just no way.

The alternatives are separate formal portraits or simply going with candid shots. These kinds of touchy situations are a good reason to provide a disposable camera on each table. They're fun because amateur photographers have been known to produce some absolute gems. You can purchase disposables at camera shops and discount stores for about $13.00 for 24 exposures. Developing the photos is an extra cost.

Stepping In or Out?

The best time to speak with your mother, father, and stepparents about the wedding pictures is while you are planning all of the other details. It's easier to resolve the photographs issue early on than to continue worrying about how the pictures will be handled. Without advance agreement, you face the probability of anger, awkwardness, or just plain embarrassment on your wedding day.

According to one wedding consultant, "If your mother or father is remarried, it is considerate to include the new spouse in family photographs." Your stepparent does not need to be included in all formal family photographs, but a number of shots are generally called for. Two popular choices are a shot of the bride or groom

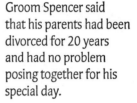

One photographer told me, "I've shot many formal photographs that included everyone— biological and stepparents in the same portrait."

Groom Spencer said that his parents had been divorced for 20 years and had no problem posing together for his special day.

Since the wedding is only going to happen once, I suggest that you include the following formal photographs in your list:

1. Bride and groom

2. Wedding party (bride, groom, attendants)

3. Bride with mother, stepfather, and siblings (biological and steps from this side of the family)

4. Bride with father, stepmother, and siblings (biological and steps from this side of the family)

5. Groom with mother, stepfather, and siblings (biological and steps from this side of the family)

6. Groom with father, stepmother, and siblings (biological and steps from this side of the family)

alone with his/her parent and stepparent, and another photo including the parent and stepparent with the newlywed couple.

To avoid conflict on this question, bride Daria opened up the discussion early: "I gave a picture list ahead of time to everyone and asked for their comments." The entire family reached agreement on the appropriate formal pictures. Unfortunately, in her case, the best laid plans went astray. Her stepsisters were unintentionally left out of the formal portraits. The lesson here: Don't forget to give the photographer a complete list of all shots you really want to have in your album.

Out of Sight

If your mother or father is escorted by a casual date, it is not appropriate for this guest to appear in your formal family wedding photographs. The person will have opportunities to appear in candid pictures.

One photographer told me of a wedding where neither the bride's father nor the bridegroom's father appeared in any of the formal photographs. It turns out that both of these fathers had very little involvement in the rearing of their children and were invited to attend the wedding as guests only.

For Posterity

"I have a personal feeling that, if at all possible, a portrait should be taken of the bride and groom with their biological parents," another wedding consultant advises. "This goes in the album for history's sake, to be passed down to the grandchildren." My recommendation is to recognize that divorced parents may not wish to be pictured as a couple. I cannot stress too much the sensitivity of this issue.

Family circumstances and moods change. For the sake of speed, ask each parent to gather his or her picture group of family members together while pictures (1) and (2) are being taken. Then you and your groom can move right into the groups that are already arranged and standing nearby watching the photographer.

If you and your new husband both want to appear in the combination family photographs (3) through (6), be ready to hop right into the scene and avoid long delays trying to get everyone else together again.

If the photo session is going smoothly and rapidly, consider including grandparents in the pictures with you and their daughter or son (your mom or dad) for a three-generation memento. Otherwise, these may be taken as candid shots.

After talking with a large number of people, I find that the consensus is, "When in doubt, shoot." This way, no one will get their feelings hurt because they are excluded. By taking advantage of all photo opportunities, everyone participating will have choices. Remember, you don't have to select all of the pictures in the package. As for candid shots, if you find a picture offensive, you can always tear it up and throw it away—or pop it into the mail to the person the photographer captured.

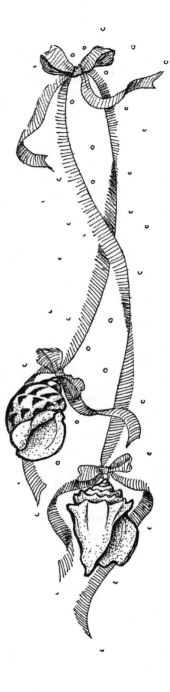

There is no surprise more magical
than the surprise of being loved:
It is God's finger on man's shoulder.

— Charles Morgan

Command Performances

A side from the wedding ceremony itself, there are a few rituals that take place and serve to highlight the main event. They include bridal showers, the rehearsal dinner and the wedding reception. Indeed, the receiving line at the reception is a memorable custom where the bride and groom once again have a chance to thank guests for sharing their special day.

Showers

According to old, old traditions, you can't marry until you prove that you're valuable. Today that means you must be loaded with stuff that represents the modern version of a dowry—blenders, pickle forks, towels, and candlesticks. In truth, many brides today accumulate many of the household items they need to start a new life with their husbands by having showers before their weddings.

Bridal showers are a time for friends and family members to meet in intimate gatherings to celebrate the wedding. They also provide the opportunity for friends and family to get to know one another better before the wedding.

Coed showers, often held in the evening after work, have become very popular. They fit with the lifestyle of today's bride and bridegroom. This idea has been a boon for hardware store bridal registries.

Rain Drops

It is not socially correct for a shower to be hosted by a member of either the bride's or bridegroom's immediate family. A close friend or member of the bridal party is the proper hostess for a bridal shower. Parents or brothers and sisters are always welcome to help with the planning and expenses but they do not issue the actual invitation.

Stepparents may give a luncheon or reception in your honor but not an event that is characterized by the giving of presents. Miss Manners phrases it clearly, "One is not supposed to be greedy on behalf of a relative." Stepparents are considered immediate family.

The secret of many wedding successes is beginning to sound like a broken record. "If at all possible, invite all family members who show an interest in sharing events with you."

Some families have told me about showers (and other wedding parties) that included stepmothers and stepsisters at all female parties with stepfathers and stepbrothers joining the coed parties. According to bride Wendy, "We had smaller showers in the towns and cities where different family members lived. My mom and stepmom were invited to every one even though they weren't able to attend each party."

If potential adversaries accept the invitation, they are expected to "behave." If they feel their presence would be terribly awkward, they are usually sensitive to the feelings of others and frequently decide on their own to "stay away."

Beverly says,

I heard about a great way to share photos of the wedding. One stepmother took the pictures from the table cameras and made up collages on 11x17 paper. She took them to a copy shop and made color copies of the sheet. She made several versions according to the divisions in the families. This way, everyone was comfortable showing off pictures. She kept the master pictures in an album and can have a selection made up any time.

Wedding Rehearsal

This mock ceremony covers all of the basics. Regardless of whether the ceremony is held in a house of worship or some other location, the officiant(s) will walk you through the physical paces of the formal ritual. Wedding planning books will give you an idea of what to expect in terms of where people walk, sit, and stand according to religious or traditional guidelines.

When there's a divorce in the family, it's a good idea to discuss any extenuating family circumstances with your officiant. Your preferences for arrangements that digress from the traditional might need special approval. There may also be religious restrictions about format changes. Flexibility is an important factor in selecting both your officiant and the site.

Your minister, priest, rabbi, or justice of the peace needs to know about parent divorces and remarriages for another reason. In the unlikely event that performing a wedding for such a family is a new experience, he or she will have time to obtain the necessary education in protocol.

One minister I interviewed was not prepared in advance and said, "I had no idea how to handle a stepmother. I didn't know where she was supposed to sit or even who should escort her to her seat. My wife wasn't able to help me because she had been a nun for thirty years."

The Mothers

The wedding rehearsal may be the occasion of the first meeting between the mothers and stepmothers. Mothers admit that they worry about stepmothers trying to usurp their role as mother–of–the–bride. This mother's comment is typical, "I was scared that she (stepmother) would expect to be treated as my daughter's mother."

With the exception of an occasional nasty skirmish, mothers generally find stepmothers are quite understanding about the potential conflict. Stepmothers who have their own children are often the most sensitive to these problems. They want to behave just as they hope their own child's stepmother would behave if the roles were reversed.

Families waste a lot of time worrying when they fail to discuss these "mother issues" early in the planning stages. Given the typically satisfactory outcome, couples and their various mothers often say, "I wish we had talked about this sooner."

The Rehearsal Dinner

The rehearsal dinner is a social event for the family, wedding party and officiants. Within the last generation, it has become a customary way for the groom's family to contribute a special event for the wedding. It relieves the bride's family of some responsibility and financial burden.

As it turns out, brides and grooms report stories about virtually every combination of parents contributing toward the expenses of the rehearsal dinner. Among older wedding couples, the bride and groom usually assume all responsibility for this event.

When parents and stepparents pay for the evening, the most common method is for funds to go into the wedding pot to be distributed as needed. One groom described his situation this way: "I put the restaurant tab on my own charge card. When the bill came in, each of my parents paid half. My mother gave me the up–front room deposit and that was deducted from her half."

The rehearsal dinner does present another potential snag. It is customary for all parents to attend and that may raise issues of who is being treated better or who is being slighted. It may sound trite, but communication about the plans can head off a lot of minor problems.

Solutions I've seen range from "all parties are for everyone" to extremely sensitive cases where a parent or stepparent "quietly declines the invitation."

One family planned the rehearsal dinner at home with an open invitation. Putting all the steps and exes together in comfortable surroundings broke the ice.

The host(s) whose home is being used for this kind of gathering issues an informal invitation to the other family members. This may be done by phone or in a short note. The personal invitation reassures exes and stepparents that they are welcome.

If you are holding the event in a restaurant, round tables avoid hierarchy and the possibility of someone feeling as if he or she was put down at the end—in Siberia. This makes it possible to seat family groups comfortably at separate tables. Tactfully arranged place cards also help to skirt possible rough spots.

At times like these, it's wonderful to see the ways in which families can be surprisingly openhearted. One young boy was just about bowled over when his stepfather offered a special toast for welcoming him into his family.

A happy groom related a particularly heartwarming tale. "My father told a 'peace' story. He knew that my mother had always blamed him for being away while she was in the hospital delivering me. He apologized to my mother. My mom cried as she accepted his apology."

Opportunities for healing hurts may come at the darndest times!

Cannot be parted nor be swept away

From one another once you are agreed

That life is only life forevermore

Together wing to wing and oar to oar.
— Robert Frost

Beverly says,

If the groom's family are rather shy and feel uncomfortable meeting and greeting guests during the reception, consider asking a step-parent or sibling to fill the role. At one wedding I attended the bride's stepmother, who was at ease with strangers, graciously introduced everyone and helped explain who belonged to who allowing the birth mother to take the limelight as the bride's mother.

Receiving Line

You, your groom, and your families all want to greet guests who attend the wedding. If you start to get in a real dither about receiving lines and who–stands–where–next–to–whom, remember your primary objective. You want to welcome each guest and thank him or her for coming to share your special day! However you manage to accomplish that goal will be just fine with or without a receiving line.

With so many opportunities for adults to greet each other throughout the day, I marvel that anyone still endures the tedium of long receiving lines. In fact, I was told by a number of caterers that extended receiving lines are out of fashion because people don't like waiting for the festivities to begin. Lengthy pauses can be a damper on the party.

"Hello" Young Lovers

The receiving line issue gets complicated if you don't recognize the wedding is in two parts, the ceremony and the reception party, and the receiving line etiquette that applies to both.

Hosts of the reception are members of the receiving line at the reception. Sponsors of the ceremony are part of formal or informal

receiving lines for that portion of the wedding. This may be outside of the house of worship or within the ceremony site if it is at a hotel, home, or garden.

You should not receive guests formally at a place where you are not the host or hostess, namely a religious ceremony in a house of worship. Clergy, alone, may receive people after a religious service.

I have observed that it is becoming almost commonplace for receiving lines to begin forming within the house of worship. This is not appropriate. If you feel that it is your only choice, please discuss the idea in advance with your officiant.

This restriction does not rule out having your sponsor-parents greet guests after they have left the house of worship. They will be in position to do this along the front walk because they will be among the first to leave the seating area. This option works particularly well when the ceremony sponsors and the reception hosts are not the same individuals. It also helps if the weather cooperates.

Your hosts for the reception will extend their formal greetings at the party. At least one host should be stationed at the entrance to the party area for introductions and to shake the hand of each guest upon arrival.

If you are having a sit-down meal, the reception host(s) can

Beverly says,

At another wedding, there were so many branches to the family that the bride and groom made up name tags for the reception with family connections identified and for their friends they put "no relation at all!" The guests all rose to the occasion and added comments on their name tags like "first met bride when two hours old," etc.

- Divorced parents do not stand next to each other in the receiving line, even if they get along well. While it may not be uncomfortable for them, it surely will be confusing to some of the guests.

- If both of your divorced parents really want to be part of the receiving line, you and your new husband can stand between them.

There's a fairly easy out for this confusing situation. Fathers don't traditionally stand in wedding receiving lines. They usually circulate among the guests.

greet guests and then assist them in locating their place cards. People are more comfortable meandering around and chatting with others after they have found their seats.

Additional greeters may certainly join the host at the front entrance to form a receiving line. You, your new husband, and your bridesmaids may join the line to extend a welcome and accept best wishes. This kind of formal receiving line works best with smaller weddings where the queue doesn't stretch too far and take too long. Alternatively, the bride and groom can circulate among the guests during the party to extend their greetings. After you have greeted each guest waiting in line, the receiving line is disbanded.

If inclement weather does not permit greetings outside the house of worship immediately after the service, your ceremony sponsors will mingle informally with guests at the reception party. This provides them with the opportunity to make introductions and visit.

The ceremony sponsors participate in the reception receiving line only if they are also joint hosts of the party.

Stepping or Tiptoeing?

Stepfathers tend to be a less troublesome than stepmothers when it comes to receiving lines. If a stepfather wants to be in the receiving line with his wife, he can usually do so without stirring up controversy. Turf debates are more often the domain of mothers and stepmothers.

I've observed that even when the bride or groom is reared by a stepmother, the stepmother is often expected to stay out of the way. I can't help going back to bride Annie's differentiation between a mother or father and a parent—a biological happenstance versus a nurturing commitment. Sons and daughters of divorced mothers and fathers instinctively understand this reality. It's usually the older folks who have the hardest time facing the distinction between the two.

In the final analysis, stepparents quite properly may be included in the receiving line at the request of the bride and groom. If your parents are flexible, it's pretty much your call.

Ultimate Solution

A number of families ignore planning for the receiving line and leave its formation to chance. Or out of sheer frustration, some decide to forgo any variation of the receiving line altogether. Most families work things out somewhere between these two extremes. Couples usually want to do what will make the majority of people feel the most comfortable.

The best of all worlds is when everybody is willing to work together. This allows you to coordinate the ceremony and the reception for a cohesive day. Each segment has its own sponsors or hosts with clearly defined areas of responsibility and authority to be shared with you and your groom.

Whether or not you ultimately decide to have a receiving line, make certain that you and your new husband greet each and every guest personally during the wedding day.

The truth (is) that there is only one terminal dignity— love. And the story of love is not import—what is important is that one is capable of love. It is perhaps the only glimpse we are permitted of eternity.

— Helen Hayes

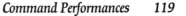

Etiquette books and wedding planners each recommend a slightly different order of events for the reception. The following sequence works well when you are trying to minimize your family's divorce-and-remarriage stress:

- Guests arrive; check coats; sign guest book

- Guests greet hosts and wedding party in the reception receiving line

- Guests locate their seats; nibble and mingle

- Music signals guests to be seated as newlyweds begin first dance

- Parents dance with newlyweds; open dancing from then on

- Everyone eats and drinks; dancing between courses

- Toasts begin

The Reception

By the time the wedding day arrives, everyone involved has a good idea about how smoothly the event will go. When there has been a divorce and remarriage in the family, each member feels either "In" or "Out" of the festivities. The wedding day is anticipated with excitement, dread, or something in-between. The degree of supportive communication and joint planning is the strongest indicator of how well things will go on your special day.

Most of the good cheer expressed throughout the wedding day is genuine. To be sure, some of the social connections may be hard to believe but most divorced parents and other aggrieved family members rediscover the humanness in each other.

I love the story about the mother who looked gorgeous after losing weight—and she knew it! Her daughter proudly said, "My mom felt confident and pretty. She was introducing my father and stepmother to everyone!"

The Master of Ceremonies

After spending months agonizing over getting the wedding just right:

the announcement . . . just right

the invitation . . . just right

the dress . . . just right

the rehearsal . . . just right

the family to behave . . . just right

. . . some brides and grooms neglect to plan the longest segment of the festivities.

Every plan leading up to the wedding day is unique to your tastes and family circumstances. And yet, when friends and family are finally gathered together, the elegant atmosphere you worked so hard to obtain may be blown away—if you let it.

I've watched couples let, or even request that, a member of the band assume responsibility for the timing and sequence of events for the reception. This is usually a person who knows nothing about the members of the family or their guests!—who uses a cookie-cutter format for each wedding reception! In the hands of a virtual stranger, your reception could become just like every other wedding reception the guests have attended within the past few years.

All of the charm and intimacy of a wedding is completely lost with the addition of a Master of Ceremonies who acts as if he is directing a three-ring circus.

One unsavory routine in the M.C.'s repertoire is to herd family members on stage, expecting them to march to a drum beat while announcing the family relationships. Trying to fit divorced and remarried families into these public credits makes for unnecessary headaches. Parents and stepparents are very sensitive to feelings of being "In" or "Out" of the family. It is not in good taste to deliberately cause family members or your guests to be uncomfortable.

My feeling is that personal introductions are much more graceful. Formal receiving is done following the ceremony and as guests enter the reception area. Family members and guests have an opportunity to mingle with each other throughout the festivities. On such a happy occasion, encourage your family and friends to meet and greet some of the guests they may not know well.

If you want an M.C. to help you coordinate the various activities throughout the reception, work with this person in advance to prepare the sequence of events, the time frame for

- ❦ Newlyweds move among the tables for greetings and photos
- ❦ Newlyweds cut the wedding cake
- ❦ Newlyweds prepare to leave: bouquet and garter toss; change into "going away" clothes; say goodbye to parents and wedding party
- ❦ Guests depart

Usually with some
careful thought and
planning there is a
sensible way of
distributing your family
so that they are not likely
to be insulted by their
seating arrangement or
by one another.

each event, and the appropriate music. Then announcements about cake cutting, bouquet throwing, and so forth, will go with the flow.

I have a major pet peeve about the music at most wedding receptions. When the band is very loud, the musical din ruins the most delightful aspect of the reception. Your reception is an opportunity for old and new friends to have conversations with you and with each other. When it's hard to be heard without yelling, your guests are reduced to sitting helplessly and simply staring around or even having to put their hands over their ears to provide relief from the loud noise. Please find musicians who know how to provide background as well as dance music.

Receiving Line at the Reception

When the ceremony sponsors and the reception hosts are the same individuals, it is often easiest to have the receiving line held at the beginning of the reception instead of immediately after the ceremony.

When the sponsors and hosts are not the same individuals, these people will greet guests at their separate functions.

You and your new husband may participate in either or both of the receiving lines. You will also circulate informally greeting each of your guests.

Reception Seating

Seating at the reception does not necessarily pose a problem. Divorced mothers and fathers are not in the limelight for this event. They do not sit at the head table with members of the wedding party.

The typical arrangement is to give each set of parents their own table. The parents' tables are positioned in front of the bridal party table on the same level as all other guest tables.

Hosting Tables

Seating at the parent tables is determined in the usual social fashion. Spouses are seated together. This means that your mother and stepfather host one parent table and your father and stepmother host another. If your mother and father have not remarried, their escorts can join them at their parent table.

Grandparents and those siblings not in the wedding party are seated with their immediate family member, your mother or father. When this head count does not fill a table, extended relatives or close friends are invited to join them.

There's a wonderful way to avoid putting siblings on the spot about which parent's table to join. You can provide a table for older brothers and sisters to host. This is a nice alternative for your biological and step siblings. The table(s) can be placed with the parent grouping or, if they prefer, closer to the band.

You may decide to have open seating for everyone except the wedding party. This works best when the meal is served buffet style and for outdoor receptions. By the way, buffet style is great for allowing people to find their own comfortable groupings, especially important when there is family friction. Buffets may be a less expensive way to provide food because you eliminate the costs of waiters and waitresses for each table.

Even when the wedding is a very formal affair, wedding consultants encourage all family members to get up and socialize with each other and the rest of the guests. People invited to the reception do spend most of their time nibbling on hors d'oeuvres, dancing, and visiting. Sitting at tables is primarily for eating the meal and resting the feet. Just make sure that comfortable seating is readily available for your elderly and physically handicapped guests.

Florist Athena described a two-tiered head table variation. "The bridal party was on the upper level; parent tables were on the lower level. Both the bride's and the groom's parents were divorced and remarried so there were four parent tables."

When you have a father and a stepfather attending the reception, you have choices. You can:

- dance only with your father
- dance only with your stepfather
- dance with each father
- skip the father dance

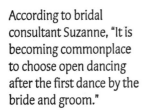

According to bridal consultant Suzanne, "It is becoming commonplace to choose open dancing after the first dance by the bride and groom."

Newlyweds Janice and John dedicated a song to his mother and stepfather. They had supported the bridal couple through some very difficult times while planning the wedding.

Bride Lorraine raised her glass to her stepfather saying, "Thank you for being my parent—for being there when I called home to talk; for treating me with as much love and affection as you do your own daughters."

This is a perfect opportunity for you and your new husband to thank your family, bridal party, and guests for sharing the wedding with you. And, with that gracious departure, go . . . and have a wonderful time on your honeymoon!

At the End of the Rainbow

The first dance is reserved for the newlyweds. The eyes of every guest will be upon you. This is not the time to stand center stage, in a bear hug, shuffling your feet. Take dancing lessons long enough to learn how to waltz. It looks and feels spectacular when you're in formal attire. Call local dance studios to find one that offers classes or individual instruction to ease you and your fiancé through first dance jitters.

Traditionally, the second dance is reserved for you and your father. The band plays "Daddy's Little Girl," unless, you have two daddies, and this makes the situation awkward. Then, you may want to forgo this part of the dancing.

This decision does not have to be made until the very end of the planning period. Chances are that it will be made for you by the degree of involvement of each father and how well everyone is getting along.

There is precedent for eliminating the father dance. Wedding consultant Lauren advised, "Most couples with divorced parents skip this convention."

If there is to be a father–daughter dance, be sure to drag him into the dance studio for a brush up on his footwork, unless he's already a wonderful dancer. You will still be the focus of interest for your guests.

Sidestepping

When you have a number of parents and stepparents, you may prefer to select a musical medley so that you and your groom dance briefly with each parent, changing partners whenever there is a song change.

By having a family dance, either after the father–daughter dance or in place of it, you will be setting the mood for guests to get up and join the group on the dance floor. This is the signal for open dancing to begin and it continues throughout the reception.

Whatever you decide to do, be sure to let your bandleader know. Also make time to coordinate the music and the length of each song for the initial family dances. Sometimes these dances drag on so long that both dancers and guests fidget.

At this point, parents toast the newlyweds and the newlyweds toast the parents. When you and your new husband have a lot of mothers and fathers at the reception, it is necessary to give your best man a list of parent names in the preferred sequence. Ask your parents beforehand who would and would not like to offer a toast. Avoid embarrassing anyone.

When parents have completed their toasts, the floor is open to the wedding party and guests. Toasts may continue, off and on, for as long as people choose to offer public good wishes. It is during this time period that E-mails, faxes, and cards are read aloud by the best man.

The Newlyweds

After you have finished your meal and the toasts are over, it is time to circulate among the guest tables. This is an opportunity for you to ask the question or make the comment that was forgotten in the rush of the receiving line. It's also a chance for amateur photographers to take special candid close-ups.

When you have completed your rounds, proceed to the ritual of cutting the wedding cake. After the cake ceremony, your travel schedule and timing arrangements with the caterers begin to control the festivities. Gauge your timing accordingly so you do not have to rush through the bouquet and garter toss, changing clothes, or locating each member of your wedding party and family to say goodbye.

Toasts

Toasts and dedications are a great opportunity to let special people know just how special they are to you. This custom is an important part of the rehearsal dinner and wedding reception. In the interest of keeping events moving gracefully, it's a good idea to keep the wedding day toasts short.

The best man begins the toasts at a comfortable point during the meal. He decides when to begin and orchestrates this portion of the reception. He uses the following order for the first three toasts:

- Best man toasts the bride
- Groom toasts the bride
- Bride toasts the bridegroom

Grace & Arthur's Story

"Why can't even one thing about planning this wedding be easy?" a frustrated voice cried out as its owner swept into my office. Peering down at me, quite obviously expecting an answer, was a tall, slender brunette in her mid 20's—with blazing eyes on the verge of dripping tears.

"I didn't necessarily expect my wedding day to be the happiest day of my life, but I didn't think that my parents' divorce twelve years ago would make such a mess of things for me now."

This was Grace Straus speaking. She was eleven years old when her parents made the decision to divorce. Both her mother and father had remarried. Grace was having a devil of a time figuring out how to make wedding plans with her four parents.

To make matters worse, the groom, Arthur Jones, also had parents who were divorced and remarried. Between Grace and Arthur there were eight parents and numerous siblings, half siblings and step siblings. Grace and Arthur would be the first children in either family to wed. They would be the "trial run" for their brothers and sisters.

When they began planning their wedding, Grace and Arthur had felt completely overwhelmed at the prospect of trying to fit their complex families into a traditional wedding format. Who would pay for what? Who should sit where in the church? With the family scattered all over the country, how could they plan a wedding that wouldn't exclude anyone? "At first, I seriously considered eloping," said Grace. "Fortunately, Arthur was more positive. He knew I had always dreamed of a beautiful wedding and he encouraged me to 'go for it.'"

Here is how Grace and Arthur accomplished their dream wedding, by making thoughtful decisions, one at a time.

OPENING LINES

When Grace and Arthur decided that the time was right to make their big announcement, they wanted to break the news in person if possible. "Grace decided to wait and tell her mother and stepfather, Margaret and Richard, until our vacation visit with them in New York at the end of August," said Arthur. "After that, we were heading back to Charleston for the beginning of Grace's second year of graduate school."

"To even things up, we called Arthur's father and stepmother, Malcolm and Rosalie, and made arrangements to visit with them in Chicago," said Grace. We cut our New York trip short by a couple of days so we could tell them in person too."

While in New York, Grace called her father and stepmother, Jacob and Adeline, at their home in San Francisco. She told them about her engagement and the tentative idea of having the wedding the following August. She invited both of them to visit in Charleston during his next business trip to the area.

Arthur called his mother and stepfather, Alma and Joseph, at their vacation home in Maine. They were delighted with the news and, since both mothers were friends, made plans to drive down to New York the following weekend for a brief visit before Grace and Arthur left for Chicago.

Immediately following the couple's Chicago visit, Malcolm and Rosalie Jones wrote to Grace's mother and stepfather. The letter spoke of their pleasure at having Grace become a member of their family and their desire to entertain the couple at a party in Chicago after the wedding.

THE OFFICIAL ANNOUNCEMENT

Grace had lived with her father and stepmother for the first few years following her parents divorce. A change in family circumstances resulted in a permanent move to her mother's home and a period of estrangement from her father and stepmother. Following her mother's remarriage, Grace continued to feel that "home" was with her mother and stepfather, even while she was away at college. Now that she had her own apartment, "home" for holidays or vacations, and for comfort and security, still meant being with her mother and stepfather.

While she got along with her father and stepmother, they had limited contact. Grace and Arthur decided to word their engagement announcement like this:

Mr. and Mrs. Richard Burr O'Brien announce the engagement of her daughter, Miss Grace Louise Straus to Mr. Arthur Hamilton Jones of Boston. Miss Straus is also the daughter of Mr. Lou Jacob Straus of San Francisco. The bridegroom's parents are Ms. Alma Jones Rizzo of Boston and Mr. Malcolm Conrad Jones of Chicago.

SEPARATE EVENTS PLANNED

The couple and their families were spread all over the map.

"At first it seemed that the fact of our families being so far-flung was a liability in planning this wedding," Arthur said. "Then we suddenly realized we could turn geography to an asset by planning separate events." Feeling that all of the parents could be reasonably comfortable together for brief periods of time, they decided that was "good enough" and encouraged each set of parents to plan a portion of the wedding festivities and assume responsibility for related expenses. Their primary request was that all parents be invited to all events. The parents could then choose whether or not to attend.

"I really wanted to have our ceremony in a small chapel near my mother's and stepfather's home in New York City," Grace said. "My mom and stepdad sponsored it and assumed expenses of the ceremony and my wedding dress. Since I overspent on my gown, I also made a contribution to the ceremony.

All parents were invited to attend the ceremony as honored guests. Grace's father and stepmother offered to host (and pay for) the reception to be held immediately following the wedding service. They set a time and place to meet with Grace and Arthur to discuss details and together they planned an intimate gathering of extended family and close friends. "Since the reception was going to be 'out-of-town' for my father and stepmom, I actually made most of the arrangements, discussing options with them by phone."

"My folks wanted to have a second reception in Chicago when we returned from our honeymoon," Arthur said. "After all, I had lived with my father and stepmother before going off to college. My parents were ecstatic about the wedding and thrilled to be able to show us off. They discussed general plans with us but actually made the arrangements pretty much independently. They told us that our job was to 'show up and be happy.'" This large party included Arthur's high school friends as well as all extended family members and special friends of the bridal couple.

Arthur's mother and stepfather offered their vacation home for the honeymoon, including travel expenses.

The whole gang in married-student housing in Charleston made plans for a casual (and inevitably rowdy) party to mark the couple's new legal status. It included the college crowd and was held right before classes started in the fall. Grace and Arthur chipped in to help pay for the beer and wedding cake.

SPECIAL ATTENDANTS

When Grace and Arthur made the decision to have a fairly small wedding, they avoided a number of potentially difficult decisions in selecting members of the wedding party.

Grace has one biological sister, one stepsister and one stepbrother. "I was planning to ask my stepsister, Sara, to be in the wedding, but when finally I asked her she confessed that she had just found out she was pregnant. She regretfully declined due to anticipated girth." Grace invited her sister, Jenn, to be her maid of honor. She selected Arthur's younger sister, Ann, and her best friend, Silvana, to be her bridesmaids.

Arthur has one biological sister, one biological brother, and one half brother. Arthur invited his brother, Temple, to be his best man. He selected his half brother, Larry, and his fraternity buddy, Karl, to be the ushers.

YOU'RE INVITED

Grace and Arthur decided that a relatively small wedding would work out best for them. The ceremony would take place in the small chapel where Grace had attended periodically as a child—and where she participated in Christmas Eve services faithfully every year. Grace's long, white gown set the tone; attire would be formal.

The reception would be a dinner at The Hermitage in Central Park. Because of geography, the reception would be small. Not only did their parents live all around the country, their high school and college friends did also, and the graduate school group couldn't afford to travel to each other's weddings.

Whoever couldn't get to New York could attend the separate reception in Chicago or the party thrown by student friends in Charleston. Since everybody was well-covered (all family and friends would be invited to at least one celebration), they eliminated the idea of sending wedding announcements.

The couple set the number of attendees for the ceremony at approximately sixty people. Their parents each limited their lists to family members and one couple from a social friendship. Although they knew it wasn't necessary to invite dates for single guests, Grace and Arthur decided that each unmarried member of the wedding party should be given the option of inviting a companion. They did not include "and guest" on invitations for other single family members.

The bridal couple created their own list of friends to receive invitations and these guests rounded out the total number invited to the wedding. "We each called or wrote to our own family members with youngsters and explained that we could only invite children over the age of eight," Grace said.

WORDING OF THE INVITATION

Grace and Arthur found that decisions about issuing invitations and wording were fairly easy once the when-and-where questions were answered.

Grace's mother and stepfather issued the invitations:

Mr. and Mrs. Richard Burr O'Brien
request the honour of your presence
at the marriage of her daughter
Grace Louise Straus
to
Mr. Arthur Hamilton Jones
on Wednesday, the twenty-ninth of July
One thousand nine hundred and ninety-four
at four o'clock
St. Paul's Church
Park Avenue
Baltimore, Maryland

Grace's father and stepmother offered to pay for the reception dinner, including the invitations to the event. They offered the couple a reasonable budget. Expenses beyond that amount had to be negotiated. Grace and Arthur agreed to assume responsibility for making the arrangements with the restaurant.

This is what the reception invitation looked like:

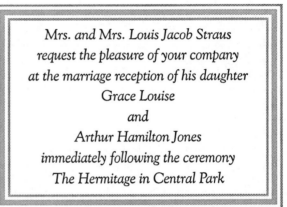

Mrs. and Mrs. Louis Jacob Straus
request the pleasure of your company
at the marriage reception of his daughter
Grace Louise
and
Arthur Hamilton Jones
immediately following the ceremony
The Hermitage in Central Park

This invitation was enclosed in the envelope with the ceremony invitation. Grace's mother's New York home was the return address for RSVPs for both wedding and reception. Her mom let her stepmother know the head count for the reception dinner. For all practical purposes, Grace and her mother dealt with the restaurant although Grace discussed choices and costs with her father and stepmother. "Things are always a bit strained between my parents," Grace said. "My mother and father did not communicate directly with each other about dinner plans. My father just wrote the checks for deposits and the final payment."

Malcolm and Rosalie Jones, Arthur's father and stepmother, wanted to "show off" the newlyweds to all of their friends. While this second event was part of the wedding festivities as far as the family was concerned, all plans for this party were made independently of those for the wedding day.

Malcolm and Rosalie sent this invitation:

To celebrate the recent marriage of
Grace Louise Straus
and
Arthur Hamilton Jones
Mr. and Mrs. Malcolm Conrad Jones
request the pleasure of your company
at a Cocktail-Buffet
on Saturday, August thirty-first
from six to eight-thirty o'clock
The Landmark Club
Chicago

Arthur's mother and stepfather maintained close contact with Grace's mother and stepfather. They enjoyed being part of the discussions and planning. While Alma and Joseph were included in the excitement, participated in a number of the planning

sessions, and made a handsome contribution to the honeymoon, they were neither sponsors of the ceremony nor hosts of the reception. Their names did not appear on either of those invitations.

Each parent and stepparent was invited to each wedding event as an honored guest.

DOWN THE AISLE ON WHOSE ARM?

For the first few years after her parents' divorce, Grace Straus had a close and active involvement with each of her parents. Once Grace's mother remarried, however, Jacob seemed relieved to have his responsibilities taken up by another man. While he maintained contact every now and then with Grace, her stepfather Richard became the parent she relied upon emotionally.

When Grace made the San Francisco phone call to tell Jacob and Adeline about her engagement, she was both surprised and delighted that her father wanted to participate. Over the years, she had become accustomed to his remoteness. "It's sad for me to think about dad for very long," she told me, "because it's hard for me to accept the kind of father he has been."

Grace understood that her father didn't want to be left out of the wedding even though he had not been a part of her adolescence and college years. She was also very happy that he was willing to help financially. Still, feeling a bit cold-hearted, she concluded that she did not feel really comfortable about having her father walk her down the aisle.

From the available options, Grace narrowed her aisle escort choices to four: Jacob, her father; Richard, her stepfather, Margaret, her mother; Jacob and Richard. After talking it over with Arthur and her mother and her stepfather, Grace decided that she would like to have both her father and stepfather escort her down the aisle. When she announced her wishes, both fathers were delighted to accept the honor.

Grace told me that the rehearsal was awkward and they also felt uncomfortable for the first few steps on the wedding day. After that, the three of them got into the swing of sharing the occasion when they noticed that everyone in the church was beaming.

PARTY TIME

There were three showers to celebrate Grace and Arthur's wedding. Grace helped to prepare the guest list for one of them; the other two were surprises.

Grace's mother's best friend in New York, "Aunt Sue," planned a traditional "girls' shower" for Grace that included her high school friends as well as her mother's friends. They sent invitations to her stepmother in California, Arthur's mother in Boston, and Arthur's stepmother in Chicago. Grace's stepmother and Arthur's stepmother sent regrets due to the travel distance. Alma Rizzo joined the party.

Grace and Arthur's married friends in Chicago, Gil and Nancy, gave a surprise co-ed shower for the couple when they visited with Arthur's folks at the beginning of June. It was a household shower—hardware for Arthur and kitchen gadgets for Grace. All parents and stepparents received invitations. Malcolm and Rosalie Jones and Margaret and Richard O'Brien attended.

The Charleston party was a combination shower/reception celebration given by the group in married-student housing. Grace and Arthur knew about plans for the party; they didn't know it would include gifts. The theme was "Games" and the gifts were all board, card, and group games ranging from Monopoly to a volleyball and net. Parents were invited but did not attend.

Everyone who took candid pictures gave Grace and Arthur a set of prints.

THE WEDDING PREVIEW

The church rehearsal took place at eleven o'clock Tuesday morning. Following the rehearsal, all parents and members of the bridal party gathered at Grace's mother's home for an informal buffet luncheon. The luncheon was over by about three-thirty in the afternoon and everyone was free to take care of last minute details or continue sightseeing. The younger group went on a trip to the zoo.

Margaret and Richard O'Brien, Grace's mother and stepfather, and Alma and Joseph Rizzo, Arthur's mother and stepfather, shared in the arrangements, expenses, and clean-up for the buffet lunch. They also helped to coordinate transportation, to and from the church, for the members of the bridal party.

THE WEDDING VIEW

Grace and Arthur said they felt very fortunate that each set of parents wanted to share the wedding and that all of them were reasonably comfortable being around each other. Seating for the wedding service was easily arranged.

Grace's mother and stepfather, Margaret and Richard, as sponsors of the ceremony, sat together in the second row, on the bride's side, behind the row reserved for the attendants.

Grace's father and stepmother, Jacob and Adeline, had a cordial relationship with her mother and stepfather and didn't need a "buffer" row. They sat together in the next row.

Traditionally, Arthur's mother, Alma, would have been seated in the second row, on the groom's side. However, in deference to Arthur's dad and stepmom, with whom Arthur had made his home, Alma and Joseph elected to sit in the third row.

Arthur's father and stepmother, Malcolm and Rosalie, accepted their honored seats with pleasure and sat together in the place of honor.

WELCOME

Grace and Arthur were spared any possibility of conflict about receiving lines when each set of parents chose to be closely involved with different segments of the wedding.

Margaret and Richard O'Brien, Grace's mother and stepfather, as sponsors of the ceremony, greeted guests outside of the church immediately after the nuptials. That is, they greeted guests outside until it started raining. Then, everyone dashed for cars and headed for The Hermitage in Central Park. During the reception party, the O'Brien's circulated and made sure to visit with guests they had missed during their "formal" receiving time.

Jacob and Adeline Straus, as hosts for the reception party, met and received guests near the entryway to the private dining room. Jacob stood first in line as he knew many of the guests and was able to make proper introductions to his wife.

Arthur's parents, Alma and Joseph Rizzo and Malcolm and Rosalie Jones were honored guests at the reception. They mingled and visited just as every other guest in the dining room.

Grace and Arthur had formal wedding photographs taken immediately after the ceremony. They and their attendants joined her father and stepmother in the reception party receiving line.

EAT, DRINK, AND BE MERRY

The reception immediately following Grace and Arthur's nuptial ceremony was a formal dinner. Soft harp music was played in the background throughout the evening. There was no dancing.

During the cocktail period, all guests mingled. Each set of parents assumed responsibility for seeing that no one was left out of conversations. It was a small and friendly group.

The bridal table was positioned in front of a beautiful, hand-painted mural along the back wall. The bridal party faced a glass wall of windows overlooking Central Park.

Round tables, for parents and guests, were positioned throughout the private dining room. They did not have a row of parent tables adjacent to the bridal table. Guests of all ages were seated at each table; there were no separate tables for children.

Looking back now, how do Grace and Arthur feel about their wedding? "It was everything we hoped it would be," they both agreed.

Happy Endings

For Couples Planning to Remarry

Encore Weddings

A second or third wedding is so dramatically different from a first wedding that I think it needs a totally new ritual name. Encore weddings are a family affair. The first time you spoke your marriage vows, you were bringing your family of origin into your new relationship. This time, your family of origin and your first family will need to be integrated into your new family.

You have undoubtedly already had a fair amount of life experience. There are most likely pleasant and painful memories about material possessions gained or lost, and human beings loved or resented. Even after the memories have faded, they continue to be part of your life's picture. You are going to need flexible boundaries in your new household to ease the exchange of children, money, and decision-making power. You may wish you could ignore the past, but the past never stays where you might think it belongs.

Couples tell me that they were unprepared for the complexities of remarried life. There are brand new issues to think about this time. Formerly married people develop ideas about marriage that are based upon first-time experiences. Chances are pretty good

When children are involved, the emotional aspect becomes more complex. Traditional marriage rites mark the union of a new couple. When you and your spouse have children, much more is happening. This marriage is the union of a new family.

that you and your bridegroom each have assumptions about this new marriage that you may or may have not discussed with each other. If you don't talk about your feelings, you could become resentful over things your new spouse hasn't even thought about. It's not possible to deal with problems if one of you doesn't know they exist!

For instance, who will be the "kin-keeper" in your new family by doing such things as remembering birthdays and maintaining the holiday card address list? In a first marriage, women have traditionally assumed this role. Is this an appropriate expectation with remarriage and the increased numbers of extended family members?

Husbands and wives may need to rethink these kinds of issues. One husband said: "Not only did I take on my wife's new relatives, but I also had to take responsibility for relationships with my own family members. Communication, birthday cards, holiday gifts—all of that was taken care of by my first wife and she doesn't do it anymore."

Enough cannot be said to encourage discussions that will provide a sound basis for a very happy encore marriage. Preparing for your marriage as well as preparing for the wedding is extremely important.

You need to review the major factors that contribute to the failure of second marriages: marrying too soon after divorce, and marrying without awareness of potential second marriage problems. For good, helpful information, write or send an E-mail to the Stepfamily Association of America, Inc., 650 J Street, Suite 205, Lincoln, NE 68508; E-mail: stepfamfs@aol.com or call (800) 735-0329. They also have a web site at http://www.stepfam.org.

"I Do"

Second and third marriages have become so common that people are attending more of their friends' remarriages than they are of their friends' children's marriages.

A second-timer told me that his teenage boys gave him a framed poster for his den. It is a print of icicles dripping down to form a scenic stream. The boys say it depicts the end of a rigid existence, leading into a new and fluid one.

Not all the world looks fondly upon middle-aged lovers. Remarriage disrupts well-established family patterns. And, while couples openly agree that sex is important in encore marriages, they are quick to add that other factors, especially care of children and economic security, are also important considerations in the decision to try again. For other family members, these matters inevitably lead to questions about motives: "Why are you doing this, Mom?" or "What does she want from you, Dad?"

Friends and family on both sides will go through a series of adjustments before feeling comfortable with the remarriage. Many children find that the transition of their parents' remarriage is more stressful than the divorce. Accepting a stepparent is not easy. Genuine love takes time. If you remarry later in life, you may wonder if there will be enough time.

Friends who were there for you through your divorce and single period may have difficulty making another transition. If some of them have shaky marriages, they may have evaluated their own options by observing your divorce experience. If they have remained in an unhappy marriage, you may be upsetting their precarious balance again by your example of finding happiness in a new relationship.

This marry-go-round continues to affirm Dr. Samuel Johnson's philosophy that remarriage is the triumph of hope over experience.

We create more contented lives by boosting our sense of humor, being more willing to let go of the unimportant, and making a conscious decision to enjoy ourselves and our partners. We finally reach a stage in our lives when we don't have to see eye-to-eye in order to walk arm-in-arm.

Self-help books, family counselors, and TV and radio talk shows offer a steady stream of guidance for picking a good mate this time. Friends and family, especially children, will give you plenty of advice. And most organized religions require pre-marital counseling sessions. Everyone agrees that serious introspection is important.

Statistics tell us that over half of divorced men and women remarry within two years after their divorce. If this is your timetable, you and your family will be experiencing the added stress of incorporating new family members while you are still struggling with the changes produced by the divorce.

Divorce is a process, not merely an event at a point in time. If you have children, you will always be dealing with their other parent. The style you develop with your ex-spouse will set the tone for future interactions. Take time to consider this: What is your style and what is your fiancé's style? Are they compatible?

Take a long, hard look at your spouse-to-be and, if possible, talk to the ex-spouse. A "lovely person" will do everything within his or her power to see that their children are cared for. What you see happening today may be the script of what your life will be like tomorrow.

Dual-career couples have too little time in first marriages. The problem becomes a potential danger zone in encore marriages that add children and an ex-spouse or two. Harried parents frequently complain about the lack of privacy and time to be alone together. "This will work out in time," is an unrealistic expectation. Very few things in life are corrected by time alone. Take time to create enough space for your new relationship to deepen and flourish.

And remember, the bottom line is this: If your potential mate admits to a problem dealing with the existence of your children, you'd better believe it. The problem will not disappear when you take your wedding vows.

It's Your Choice

For an encore wedding, there are no hard and fast rules on dress. It's up to you and your personal preference. During the American Revolution, brides sometimes wore red dresses to signify rebellion. And in Civil War times, brides often wore purple to signify mourning for lost fathers or brothers.

The white wedding dress became a mark of affluence during the Victorian era. In our century, the white dress has taken on the meaning of purity. Therefore, white is conventionally associated with a first wedding.

Encore brides most often choose off-white, deep ivory, or pastel colors rather than pure white. Even prints and florals have become popular within the past few years.

An appropriate wedding ensemble may range from a romantically feminine, lacy dress of mid-calf or ankle length to an elegant suit. What you choose to wear will depend upon the formality of the ceremony, the time of day and, most important, what you'll feel most comfortable—and beautiful—wearing.

Style Revisions

First-time weddings revolve around the bride and her family. If this is your first wedding and your groom has been married before, social custom allows you to proceed "normally" in terms of clothing and customs. If this is an encore wedding for you, social custom imposes limitations on lavishness.

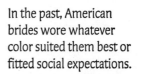

In the past, American brides wore whatever color suited them best or fitted social expectations.

A 1947 etiquette book describes additions to the ensemble for luck and happiness:

*Something old and
something new,
Something borrowed,
something blue,
And a four-leaf clover
in your shoe.*

Existing customs for encore weddings are based on first weddings. However, when the central rites of the wedding are identical to your first, it makes sense to design a new event that befits your new circumstances.

A bride in her second marriage does not wear a veil—she wants to see what she is getting into.
—Helen Rowland, Journalist, 1922

In the past, the wedding ritual publicly affirmed the new couple, but not the new stepfamily. However, there's plenty of opportunity for reworking those rituals. Marriage rites and activities can be adapted to serve the modern family's needs.

Bridal Accessories

The bridal veil is a symbol of virginity. All modern brides get away with wearing a veil for the first wedding. You will be soliciting whispers from your guests if you wear one for your encore wedding.

Beautiful alternatives are hats, ribbons, or a jeweled comb. Fresh flowers or sprigs of baby's breath are also very popular. Orange blossoms and myrtle wreaths, however, are considered emblems of virginity so they are not among your options. Choose flower blossoms that complement your outfit or are coordinated with your color scheme.

The "something blue" may be a reference to biblical days when brides wore a band of blue around the bottom of their wedding costume to symbolize fidelity and love.

Most encore brides seem to want to get rid of wedding and engagement rings from past marriages. The old engagement ring is often put in a safe for her daughter. There is "divorce jewelry" in the form of drop pendants, cocktail rings, matching diamond studs that make use of the gems and gold. Sharon had her intricate former wedding band cut in half, added new gold posts, and created "tearings."

Gift-Giving

Chances are that many of the guests you'll invite to your encore wedding gave you a generous gift for your first marriage. Your invitation tells these friends that you want them to be part of your future. They are under no social obligation to continue sending you presents if they do not attend the festivities. However, even with second or third marriages, the old rules still apply. If you attend the celebration, you send a gift. It is not in good taste to include "No Gifts" on your invitation.

In practice, invited guests usually do choose to send a small gift, whether or not they attend the ceremony. It serves as a symbol that they approve of the new union. You'll notice that friends and family avoid anything monogrammed!

Be gracious in your acceptance of presents and write your thank–you notes promptly. Your new husband has a responsibility to write his share of the notes for gifts presented to both of you. Social etiquette applies to women and men.

Gifts are often of the creative variety, such as:

- Tickets to sports events, theater productions, movies

- Special bottle of wine

- Perennial for your garden

- Restaurant gift certificate

- Exercise equipment

- A coupon for an evening of free child care

Valuable Considerations

Parents are not expected to pay for encore weddings. You and your groom are responsible for financing this event. But that doesn't mean you have to turn down offers of help from family and friends.

Many parents want to contribute in some way, most often by writing a check, preparing food for the reception, or offering their home or club for a site.

"When I told my accountant that I was getting married, he immediately handed me the name of an attorney who specializes in prenuptial agreements," Joe told me.

Most couples contemplating an encore wedding fall somewhere between financial panic and carefree disinterest. Practically speaking, it is essential that you and your intended talk about finances before you tie the knot. Failure to confront financial issues early only stalls the inevitable and may lead to big problems later on.

It's surprising how many people fear that talking about money will spoil the pre-wedding romantic atmosphere. Quite the opposite can be true. Good communication and the exchange of hard information can help to diffuse anxieties and speed up solutions to any problems that may be uncovered. Both of you

One study showed men mentioning finances as a primary concern about 15 percent of the time and women with a slightly higher 20 percent.

"My best friend always said she wouldn't marry anyone who couldn't save money for the future," Diane chuckled. "Well, she's getting married again so I asked her how much he had saved. She said, '$156.'"

"We had a homemade wedding that was more fun than the first one," one bride enthused.

should compile an inventory of your major assets and liabilities. If your previous financial management style has been "filing by piling," this is the time to get that information organized.

Why carry organization to such extremes? Because no one knows what's going to happen in the future. Big things look like little things. Little things don't have signs on them that say, "I'm going to be a big thing."

So, what about all the financial stuff that needs to be said? Are you afraid of fighting? Of uncovering irreconcilable differences? Of looking foolish because you didn't think about—or do something about—these things *before* you made plans to get married? What if only one of you believes these discussions are important and the other partner is beginning to feel, "Who needs this?"

If you are feeling intimidated and embarrassed by the thought of talking about how you will handle finances after the wedding, you're not alone. In spite of harrowing stories in the media and, perhaps from your other stepfamily friends, most people avoid the issue by denying that it's important. Discipline of stepchildren and worries over the partner's former spouse rated much more attention.

Lest we forget, however, it's a fact that money conflicts are a major contributor to divorce. Indications are that money should be at the top of the list of things to be concerned about. By the time we remarry, most of us have clearly defined money styles. Established ways of managing money affect decisions about education, housing, clothing, vacations, medical and dental services, investments, and gift giving. These concerns are not unique to step families; they are common in every marriage. In step families, however, there are usually many additional wrinkles to iron out.

Family finances will be affected by and involved in many areas of your life together. Some topics for discussion:

- Whether or not to have additional children together

- Moving away from your home town

- Quitting or starting a job

- Regular income sources

- Inheritance money

- Retirement security

- Material assets prior to marriage

- Current and potential liabilities (child/spousal support, tax liabilities, pending lawsuits, etc.)

- Diagnosed health or emotional problems

- Financial assistance to family members (children and aging parents)

- Money management styles (casual versus "bean–counting")

- How you will handle family finances (joint/separate accounts, who pays which bills, etc.)

- Insurance coverage (health, life, property, umbrella)

- Health care proxies; wills

- Income tax liability changes

You may decide to discuss special circumstances and write one letter that describes your situation and your agreement. Your signatures can be notarized and the letter will serve as a reminder of your original intentions. However, this cannot take the place of a well-considered prenuptial agreement.

Prenuptial Agreement

You may prefer to have formal conversations and hire counsel to prepare a written and legally enforceable prenuptial agreement. Ideally, each of you should be represented by a lawyer. That's the best way to be sure that the agreement will hold up if things don't work out.

There are three critical elements of a prenuptial agreement:

1. It must be signed without duress.

2. There must be full disclosure of all assets and liabilities.

3. Taken as a whole, the agreement must be fair and reasonable for both sides.

A prenuptial agreement can serve many purposes. It can:

❦ Protect the interests of the children.

❦ Protect the future rights of each spouse.

❦ Spell out ownership of property at the time of the marriage and specify who gets what at the death or divorce of a spouse.

❦ Define the financial responsibilities of each spouse during (and after) the marriage.

A prenuptial agreement cannot be expected to cover every conceivable situation and every dollar. For instance, this is not the place to write visitation arrangements for pets. A prenuptial agreement is used to establish intent and to provide broad ground rules.

Arrangements for children are increasingly being included in these agreements. Among other terms, Roberta and Tom agreed that the children will be referred to as "our boys." They would take them on one good vacation per year. Upon graduating college, they would buy each child a reasonably priced car as a present.

If your previous marriage ended in divorce, you know how many decisions were based on dollars. When things went to pieces you probably said, "Once is enough!" or "Never again!" You are making a new beginning now but you can never really lock the door on the past.

It's impossible to cross "formers" out of your life. Whether through alimony, support, or just being "out there," former spouses and their relatives constantly influence and intrude on stepfamily life—usually financially. It is clearly in the interest of both women and men to have a clear understanding of previous and future financial obligations.

Most divorced people with responsibilities to a previous family know there will be a strain on their new family. And almost all new spouses are at least somewhat aware of those prior financial obligations. But, the dollars and cents significance can never be completely clear until you start living with it.

The signing of a prenuptial agreement, or not, finally comes down to a decision you both will have to make. Discuss it openly and determine what's right for you.

Beverly says,

What To Do First

- Discuss important marital issues that you might want included in an agreement, especially assets, finances, children from previous marriages, and rights of inheritance.

- Consult a financial planner or attorney for advice. Have your agreements written in a legal contract drawn up by one or both of your attorneys.

- In your contract specify a certain time or date by which you will review or revise your contract if needed—every two to five years, for example. The contracts need not be cast in concrete.

Most money management styles are a variation on one of the following themes:

❧ "We've limited our financial expectations of each other. And therefore, we've limited our resentment."

❧ "We share the burden on issues that are our joint financial responsibility, but we handle our own accounts independently."

❧ "On most issues, we decide who is going to be the primary decision maker and who is going to be the helper. Neither of us is the same one all of the time."

Couple Talk

Separate accounts, joint accounts, or his/hers/ours accounts—there's no right or wrong way to handle the finances in a remarriage. The comfortable balance will change with the amount of money available, the length of the marriage, and evolving needs. Your initial money management system needs to be flexible, not carved in stone.

Sol and Ruth worked out a very basic agreement that was comfortable for them. He told his children, "Anything I earned before our marriage goes to you. Anything Ruth earned (she is a doctor) before our marriage goes to her children. Anything we earn from now on goes to each other—to do with as we want."

Couples often shy away from financial discussions and hope things will iron out on their own after the wedding. I look at it this way: If you've been married and divorced, you've already been through the mill and are probably lugging a lot of baggage. Some of the baggage has to do with money management but most of it is emotional—and money is tied to security. Couples who openly and honestly discuss money are participating in an act of trust, concern, and caring.

What's in a Name?

Brides are free to choose the last name they will use in marriage. Beginning around the 13th century, women first started taking their husband's last name. Among aristocratic families, women did so for prestige. There is no legal requirement to guide this decision. In the past, most women wanted the family to share a common last name. Traditionally, the name each family member uses is the husband's.

By law, you can use any name you wish, as long as it's not for illegal purposes. If you are thinking about any name variation other than taking your new husband's family name, do discuss your thoughts with him and, possibly, your children. While it is technically your choice, the consequences of your highly visible decision will have an emotional and social effect on your husband and children. Reach a mutually acceptable agreement on this issue.

Many women continue to use their former name for business and professional purposes. And often they follow tradition and take their new husband's name as their legal name.

The choice of hyphenated names does not seem to be as popular now as it was a few years ago. The reason for your choice will be highly personal. One woman told me that her mother wanted her to keep her own name—and her "independence." Dianne said, "I'm just comfortable with it. It isn't a big political statement or anything like that."

It would be interesting to know percentages of women who do and don't retain their own name. There is no easy way to find out. The logical resource, the Social Security Administration, doesn't track statistics on the number of women who apply for a name change because of marriage.

Over the past 30 years, more and more women have decided to break with tradition and keep or incorporate their own last names. This decision is based upon a variety of reasons:

- Professional status.

- Ease of spelling and pronunciation.

- Desire to keep the family name.

In addition, divorced mothers may elect not to take their new husband's name because:

- They took back their birth name following the divorce and "I've changed my name enough already."

- They decide to keep a former married name to avoid confusion for the children.

If a woman is going to use a name that differs from her husband's, the current choice seems to be her maiden name.

How Do You Want to be Addressed?

The modern lack of consistency in the matter of names and titles can lead to a lot of confusion about the proper way to address couples when writing to them. If they marry and the wife takes her husband's name the traditional form of address is correct: Mr. and Mrs. Henry James Boden. If this is not appropriate, follow the new etiquette as outlined below.

❧ A married couple, when the wife has kept her own name.

Mr. H. J. Boden and Ms. M. A. Prescott

❧ A married couple whose combined two names are too long to put on one line, use two lines. Indent the second line and write "and" followed by the wife's name.

Mr. Henry James Boden
and Ms. Marie Alma Prescott

❧ Unmarried couples, who live together but are not married, are listed on separate lines in alphabetical order. There is no "and" joining their names ("and" is used for married couples). When writing to such couples the appropriate form is as follows:

Mr. Henry James Boden
Ms. Marie Alma Prescott

You may always omit middle names or simply use first and middle initials.

Legal Affairs

Requirements for marriage licenses are determined by each state and the rules vary. In most cases, the license itself must be obtained in the county, city, or town where the marriage service will be performed. You can get information about your state's requirements by calling the city hall or county clerk's office in your area. These numbers are in the Government Section of your telephone book.

The form you fill out to obtain a marriage license will have questions about former marriages:

- ❦ How many former marriages

- ❦ Date(s) and place(s) of former marriage(s)

- ❦ Date(s) and place(s) of divorce(s)

- ❦ Name(s) of former spouse(s)

Some states require proof of divorce or a death certificate for your former spouse. If you do not already have a certified copy, one can be obtained from the Bureau of Vital Statistics in the state where the divorce or death occurred. There is a small charge for this service.

The United States government has published a series of inexpensive booklets including *Where to Write for Marriage Records* and *Where to Write for Divorce Records*. They tell you where to write to get a certified copy of an original vital record. To obtain copies of the above, write to:

> Superintendent of Documents
> Government Printing Office
> Washington, DC 20402

Beverly says,

Look in your local telephone directory under "wedding chapels and ceremonies" for ministers, male and female, licensed to conduct religious or civil wedding ceremonies.

One woman I know, a national keynote speaker, is also a member of the Church of Life. She will work with any couple to customize a wedding ceremony.

Most states have a waiting period between the time you submit the marriage license application and the time it is granted. This may be as long as five days. In most states, the waiting period can be shortened under certain circumstances. If you are planning to have the ceremony in a state or location other than your own, call ahead to inquire about their requirements. Also ask if telephone applications are permitted. You may be able to save yourself a trip.

Authorized Officiants

Couples planning an encore wedding usually opt for a ceremony that is quite different from the last go-round. If you're looking for a new twist, many couples choose to hold their encore wedding on location! Disneyland, Las Vegas, the Carribean and English castles are among the favorites. Legal requirements are mandated by the individual states and must be performed within their geographic jurisdictions.

In most states, you have a pretty big choice of who can administer your marriage vows. Once an exclusive privilege of males, there are now women and men in various capacities who can conduct a ceremony. Approval to perform a wedding service is granted by the individual states and the requirements do vary. In general, you may consider the following individuals:

- Clergy—ordained in approved state categories of the general law (in some states, clergy must also be licensed as a Justice of the Peace).

- Clergy—those not in state approved categories but who have met special requirements and filings.

- Out-of-state clergy—with special authorization.

- Judges and retired judges—elected or appointed.

- 🐝 Family support magistrates such as State Referees.

- 🐝 Justices of the Peace—some states require a solemnization appointment.

- 🐝 Town Clerks—by virtue of their office.

- 🐝 Individuals—those who have obtained a special one-time designation by the governor.

Before you make a commitment to one of these officiants, confirm his or her authority to marry you in the location you have chosen.

Beverly says,

Many couples also choose to hold their encore wedding on location! Disneyland, Las Vegas, the Carribean and English castles are favorites.

A successful marriage requires falling in love many times, always with the same person.
— Mignon McLaughlin

Religion and Encore Marriages

Obviously, you must obtain a civil divorce prior to remarriage. In addition, you must meet the requirements (blood tests, etc.) of the state in which you decide to have the ceremony. Satisfying these two issues will make you eligible for a civil ceremony. For a religious service, there will probably be additional requirements. Contact your own house of worship as soon as possible to get specific information.

You will find that most religions require an approval process, formal or informal, for an encore marriage. Officials generally try to determine if both parties are marrying freely and if there are issues lingering from their first marriages that will infringe on the new one.

The Roman Catholic "declaration of nullity" and the Jewish "get" are the two most familiar requirements for a religious sanction to an encore marriage. Other faiths have some variation of these forms.

Ecclesiastical Rulings

Most religions require an approval process, formal or informal, for an encore marriage.

The Roman Catholic Church has a firm position on remarriage for parishioners. In addition to a civil divorce, all first marriages must be declared null by the church court before a new marriage service can be performed in a religious ceremony.

One man told his priest that he did not want an annulment because, "I have three children and I certainly don't want to deny that I was married to their mother!"

It is a common misconception that a Catholic annulment dissolves a marriage. It doesn't. The church does not address the civil issues in a divorce. The church grants a religious annulment if it feels there are sufficient grounds to show there never was a sacramental marriage.

While some see this as a convenient loophole, the rule actually makes a distinction between a contract and a covenant of marriage. Whereas a civil contract can be broken, the Church says that the covenant model of marriage cannot be broken. Therefore, the question asked by the tribunal is: "Was a covenant made between two mature adults?" If it can be proven that a covenant of this type was not made, then a declaration of nullity is granted.

The average case takes about six to eighteen months to complete. There are application and processing fees based on a sliding scale. Your maximum expense will probably be around five hundred dollars.

For books and information about the process of annulment and remarriage within the Catholic Church consult your local diocese or a religious bookstore.

Biblical Ruling

The Jewish divorce, called a "get," is based upon the text in Deut. 24:1–4. The name comes from gimel, the third letter of the Hebrew alphabet, and teth, the ninth letter of the Hebrew alphabet. Therefore, the name is an acronym for the twelve line document.

You must have a civil judgment of divorce before applying for a get. You begin the paper process under the supervision of your rabbi. Grounds recognized by civil courts are accepted by the rabbinical court. The degree of cooperation between the divorced couple is the largest factor in determining how long the procedure takes. Each rabbi sets the fees for the get. The maximum expense will probably be around five hundred dollars.

For books and information on the Bill of Divorce, contact your local synagogue or your local religious bookstore.

Other Religious Considerations

Planning an encore wedding involves advance discussion on a number of issues that were not relevant to your first wedding. Before you begin to make plans for the wedding, confirm specific regulations with your chosen house of worship because there are allowable variations. Ask your religious officiant some of the following questions that relate to religious procedures, ceremony options, and other details.

- Do you have printed wedding policies?

- Is a civil divorce sufficient?

- Are there ecclesiastical rulings for annulment or divorce?

- Are there biblical rulings for divorce?

- Do we need formal or informal religious approval?

- Is there a marriage preparation course?

- Is premarital counseling available for the couple/children?

- Do you perform mixed-faith ceremonies? Is a special dispensation required?

- May we have co-officiants?

- Are there restrictions on choice of music (liturgical/secular/instruments)?

- May we personalize our ceremony rites?

- Do you have flexibility on any of the above?

Answers to these questions may result in a change of timing, location, or procedure for your upcoming ceremony.

Your religion may not have a publication describing its position on remarriages. The chart on pages 164–165 provides an overview of how the various religions address remarriage. Be sure to check with your own officiant.

You will reciprocally promise love,
loyalty and matrimonial honesty.
We only want for you this day
that these words constitute the
principle of your entire life and
that with the help of divine grace
you will observe these solemn vows
that today, before God, you formulate.
— Pope John Paul II

Relgious Rules and Procedures for Encore Weddings

● = Yes

Religion	Printed Policies Available	Civil Divorce Sufficient	Ecclesiastic Rulings	Annulment Required	Divorce Required	Biblical Ruling Divorce Required	Religious Approval Required	Marriage Preparation Required	Premarital Counseling Required	Couples	Children	Mixed Faith Marriage Allowed	Formal Dispensation Required	Co-Officiants Allowed	Music Liturgical Allowed	Secular Allowed	Instruments Allowed	Personalized Ceremony Allowed	Officiant Discretion Permitted
AME (African Methodist Episcopal)		●						●	●			●		●	●	●	●	●	●
American Baptist	●							●				●		●	●	●	●		●
Assemblies of God		●					●	●							●			●	
Charismatic	●	●					●	●	●	●					●	●	●	●	●
Christian Science	●							●										●	●
Church of Christ		●						●				●		●				●	●
Church of Christ of Latter–Day Saints: Temple "Sealing" (Mormon)					●		●	●				●	●		●	●	●	●	
Meeting House						●	●	●	●			●		●	●	●	●	●	●
Church of Scientology		●						●	●			●		●	●	●	●	●	●
Church of Nazarene		●						●	●	●	●	●		●	●	●	●	●	●
Community		●						●	●	●					●	●	●		●
Congregational		●						●	●	●	●			●	●	●	●		●
Eastern Orthodox	●		●	●	●		●		●									●	
Episcopal								●	●			●		●	●	●	●	●	●
Faith Evangelical	●	●					●		●						●	●	●	●	●
Greek Orthodox	●		●	●	●				●			●	●	●	●		●		

	Business Details	Printed Policies Available	Civil Divorce sufficient	Religious Procedures	Ecclesiastic Rulings	Annulment Required	Divorce Required	Biblical Ruling Divorce Required	Religious Approval Required	Marriage Preparation Required	Premarital Counseling Required	Couples	Children	Mixed Faith Marriage Allowed	Formal Dispensation Required	Co-Officiants Allowed	Ceremony Options	Music	Liturgical Allowed	Secular Allowed	Instruments Allowed	Personalized Ceremony Allowed	Officiant Discretion Permitted
Interdenominational			•									•		•		•		•	•	•		•	•
Jehovah's Witness		•	•						•			•	•					•				•	•
Jewish Orthodox								•	•			•						•		•			
Jewish Conservative								•	•			•						•		•			
Jewish Reform								•	•			•						•		•			
Lutheran			•									•		•		•		•			•	•	
Methodist			•						•			•		•		•		•	•	•		•	•
Nondenominational		•	•							•		•		•		•		•	•	•		•	•
Presbyterian			•							•		•		•		•		•		•		•	•
Quaker			•									•		•		•		•		•			
Roman Catholic						•	•		•			•		•	•			•				•	•
Salvation Army		•	•									•	•	•	•	•					•	•	•
Seventh Day Adventist			•									•				•		•					
Swedenborgian			•									•		•		•		•	•	•			
Unitarian Universalist		•	•							•		•	•	•		•		•	•	•		•	•
United Church of Christ			•									•		•		•		•	•	•		•	•
United Methodist			•									•		•		•		•	•	•		•	•

Family Strings Attached

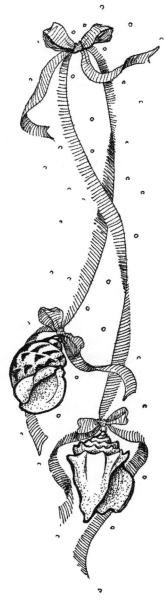

A hundred years ago parents had a lot of children. Nowadays children are apt to have a lot of parents. Getting remarried is a chance for you to start afresh. However, it is far more difficult to create an encore marriage when children are involved—and it is more important to succeed. The stakes are higher. The risks are greater. And, everybody knows it!

Everyone wants to believe that their new marriage will make things better—not only for themselves but for their children. Some may even go so far as to think that they are getting married for the sake of their children.

"The first one to get remarried gets dibs on the kids" is close to the truth according to some courts of law. One parent may see this as an advantage in arguments about who should now have the primary residence.

In the eagerness to make things better, it's easy to forget that children may have mixed feelings about the welcome and unwelcome changes that are about to occur in their lives. Trust, acceptance, and affection among new family members take time to develop. In the meantime, while your energies are focused on

For couples planning to remarry the following ideas can really help include "the family:"

Children should be the first to be told the exciting engagement news. It's best they hear it from you, and not someone else.

You and your fiancé should discuss ahead of time the type and degree of the children's participation with which you're comfortable.
Avoid disagreements and hurt feelings.

Consider including the children in the bridal party—as bridesmaids, best man, usher, flower girl, ring bearer, or other unity ceremony roles.

Ask for their help in specific areas. Take them shopping and ask their opinions.

Include the children in a "special ceremony," such as releasing butterflies, within the wedding ceremony.

your new mate, your children may feel rejected, displaced, or pushed to the periphery.

When parents announce that they plan to remarry, many say it feels more like losing one parent instead of gaining another one. It's important to realize that your new marriage, no matter how auspicious, is going to add new problems and stress to their lives along with the opportunity for satisfaction and stability.

In time, children are usually more open to adding new relatives to their collection of family members than are the adults. Stepparents are not replacements, they are an addition and go into an entirely new slot. Step grandparents are often a bonus. Most kids wouldn't dream of turning down a prospect for that position!

Teenage Children

A new marriage brings a sexual aura into the household. The newlyweds may hug and hold hands or exchange special glances and murmur "sweet nothings." They may make obvious efforts to set aside private time behind closed doors. Adolescents can be inordinately embarrassed by their parents' sexuality at a time when it's hard enough for them to manage their own newly raging hormones.

Combining unrelated, sexually mature, family members into one household raises the potential for confusion about appropriate roles. A teenage girl may wonder, "Is this attractive new boy in my life going to be my brother or a possible boyfriend?" A teenage boy may wonder if he's supposed to make romantic overtures to prove his manliness. Many adolescents are tempted to translate their curiosity, unhappiness, or frustration into romantic experimentation with similarly confused step siblings.

It is especially important to establish clearly defined boundaries in this sensitive area when you have adolescents on each side of the new family.

Discussing Your Decision

Children of all ages are concerned about the impact of a parent's remarriage on their lives. The timing of the decision and your method of announcing the news play important parts in how well the idea is received. To begin the conversation, the bride and groom should share their plans separately with their own children. Make time to meet privately with your offspring, whatever their ages, to listen to their concerns. This recognizes they may not be comfortable discussing their feelings with the future stepparent present.

Kids are often afraid of losing important family relationships (their other parent, grandparents, etc.) once you remarry. Acknowledge that divorce and remarriage do change the nature of the previous relationships but do not terminate them. Be prepared to let the children know how ongoing ties with their other family will be preserved.

Adult children tend to be particularly concerned about the status of an inheritance. Most of them expect money and property to follow a blood line, not a wedding band. Frank discussions may be in order. Mistrust, and a human tendency to think the worst, comes when there is a lack of accurate information. Neither a mother nor father needs the children's permission to marry. You do hope to have their support and best wishes.

The family history, in an encore marriage, is not starting from scratch. Children are usually self-appointed guardians of the previous family structure.

Young children are most interested in how this new situation is going to work logistically:

- Will I have to share a bedroom?

- Can I still spend as much time with my other dad/mom?

- Will you still love me as much?

Beverly says,

One California couple made telephone calls in quick succession to each of their children so they would be the ones to share the news, not a sibling.

After you have made your announcement, plan for everyone to get together and talk about the wedding. You may want to wait awhile to give the children time to adjust to the idea. The time lag could be as brief as a few hours or as long as days or weeks.

Stepparents especially need to give their new offspring time to accept them. The most successful stepparents told me that they have seen their role as similar to that of a camp counselor. They show interest and affection and provide leadership, but they let the children initiate closer bonds. The process can't be rushed and the stepparent who tries runs the almost inevitable risk of incurring hostility.

Adult Children

Parents are more likely to solicit the opinions of their adult children than younger children. And, parents listen more carefully to any objections they raise.

The responses they get are seldom impartial. Older children have many of the same emotions as younger children about their parent's remarriage. At first, they may have trouble accepting the changes your remarriage will bring.

The difference is that adult children's objections will be expressed differently and over different things. You're going to hear, "I know it's none of my business, but . . . " The issues they bring up are usually practical and financial. Sometimes they may be concerned about your judgment or your reasons for getting married again. Be prepared for their responses by deciding in advance how much you are willing to discuss with them.

I've seen children whose reactions cover the spectrum between caring and crass, selfless and selfish, generous and greedy. One family psychologist says, "I have worked with families where adults treat their parents as children, threatening not to have anything to do with the parent who remarries."

A young woman I spoke with sounded amused when she talked about the status of her engagement. "The way I understand it, his kids know he has proposed to me. Right now, they're holding confirmation hearings."

Family "Stuff"

Material issues seem to stir up the most concern with adult offspring. What will become of the inheritance, family heirlooms, and even ordinary objects that have sentimental value? Adult children are concerned about the eventual disposition of family property.

This may be a good time to talk with your children about what family objects are special to them. You can ask them about what things in your household they feel sentimentally attached to. Some of these may be duplicates that you will pack away when you merge households. If you won't be needing these items, why not offer them to your children now? They may be thrilled to have items such as old picture albums, pieces of furniture, and small kitchen appliances. Sometimes it's possible to please everyone at the same time!

Children with whom you have a good relationship deserve to know where they stand emotionally, materially, and financially, as a result of your marriage. At the same time, be sure to explain to your new spouse any commitments you have made to your children. For instance, have you told your daughter she will be inheriting your art collection? Or, does your new spouse know that you want the loan to your grandchild forgiven if it has not been repaid by the time of your death?

Commitments to other family members do not have to conflict with new love. But sometimes they do require future adjustments and, perhaps, compensations.

The Symbolism in a Name

What are the children going to call their stepparent? How will the stepparent be addressed in conversations and introductions? Will it be:

- "My mother's husband." "My father's wife."
- Your given name or nickname (Mary or Mare, Henry or Hank)
- "My stepfather." "My stepmother."
- Father or dad. Mother or mom.

The choice of name is a psychological milestone. It's a decision that is made for stepmothers and stepfathers. And, distancing names ("My father's wife") tend to become more familial ("My stepmom") as time goes by.

Allison's teenage daughter was downright nasty—not by what she said but by totally ignoring Gil. "I told her that she wouldn't be betraying her father by displaying some manners," Allison said. "I expect her to treat Gil with respect."

"I even took Jack's daughters with me when I shopped for my wedding dress but I know they really have mixed feelings," Jane told us.

My favorite story was about the couple with two daughters and one son from previous marriages. Charles and Karen said, "The kids immediately began a campaign to have us get married sooner than we were planning. One night we had a dinner of hot dogs with candlelight and music. Becca piped up, 'Isn't this romantic? Just the five of us.'"

Adult-to-Adult

Adult children wonder how they are going to establish an adult relationship with this new couple, their parent and new stepparent. How are things actually going to work at the adult level? They're wondering:

- What's expected of me if either one of you gets sick or needs help?

- Who's going to be where and when for holidays?

- Will my mom/dad still have time to help me out?

Donald voiced an observation that received a lot of affirmative nods from other parents. "My kids were actually relieved that they were no longer going to be primarily responsible for my emotional and financial well-being."

"That sounds like my son," added Donna. "He's relieved not to have to worry about me anymore."

Mark, embarking on his third marriage, said, "Don't be surprised if the relationship is fine for a while and then gets iffy. Feelings about conflicting loyalties come up again when kids realize that they actually really like you."

Mixing Feelings

During the adjustment period, most family members approach delicate issues with all of the knowledge and skill they can muster. Just remember that you can only control your own behavior; you cannot control the behavior or feelings of others. "Easy does it" is the rule of the day.

So, do your best and, good luck!

For I'm not so old, and I'm not so plain,
And I'm quite prepared to marry again.
— W. S. Gilbert

Paula and Bob decided not to live together first. They waited until the kids were ready. Their signal was this question from the children: "When are you two getting married?"

One couple decided upon a ritual for the children, ". . . an old-fashioned engagement!" They even helped his eight-year-old and her seven-year-old write a 12 page book about the wedding.

"Frankly, I was pretty bummed out about the whole thing," Fred said. "I was at college and my dad didn't tell me until I came home for Christmas. Everyone else in the family had known for weeks."

Using modern technology came in handy for one couple. They decided not to include their parents in their encore wedding and they designed a FAX to be sent to each parent the day they left for their honeymoon. As well as the announcement to soften the blow, they also invited them to a family celebration party scheduled after their return.

Telling Your Parents

Telling your parents may be more complicated this time than the first time. Surprise engagement announcements are not for parents whose lives will be adversely affected by the news. For instance, if you have been the physical caretaker of a parent and remarriage means moving to another city, it won't be easy for your parent to be thrilled by your happiness. Even if the effect will not be direct, parents have a right to be informed of the news in private. If there's any question about their reaction, it's only fair to give them a chance to air their negative feelings before having to put on a public face.

Each of you should tell your own relatives. You have a right to make an announcement. Unless you are looking for advice, don't make the mistake of phrasing the announcement as a request for permission or approval. If you do, parents may feel they have a right to help you make the decision.

In a perfect world, there would be no need for parents to struggle with the question of whether or not to verbalize concerns about your choice of a new mate. However, if they perceive you as blind with love, do they have a right or responsibility to bring up what they consider to be your intended's unsavory past, medical problems, or apparent personality defects? There is no simple answer. It's the ultimate lose–lose situation. Parents must make their own voices heard, and offspring must evaluate whether the expressions of concern are accurate or not.

After your private family conversations and blessings, arrange social get–togethers including all of your parents in order to share your plans. How many other tidbits you share will be a personal decision. Kerry worried that her new in–laws would see her as "a little shopworn. This was Dan's first marriage," she said. "It was really hard for me to tell his parents that I had been married before."

The Exes

When you have children, they and your parents are the first to know about your wedding plans. Children are natural gossips so it is courteous to speak with their other parent as soon as possible.

Paul said his conversation with his former wife, Mary, was short and sweet. "I called her to say that Cynthia and I were planning to be married in August and that we were discussing it with the children while they were with me for the weekend." He thoughtfully gave Mary time to adjust to the news before the children got home on Sunday evening.

If communication is non–existent between you and your former spouse, you can do what Carol did. "I wrote Hank a very brief note."

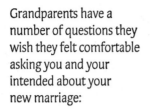

🍂 Will there be enough time/love/money to go around?

🍂 Are the children going to like you?

🍂 Do you really care for my grandchildren?

🍂 Will I see my grandchildren as often?

🍂 What kind of a stepparent are you going to be?

🍂 What are your kids like?

🍂 Will they call us "grandma" and "grandpa" too?

🍂 Do you share our religious beliefs?

🍂 Will you move away?

Your Parents as Grandparents

When you have children, your parents wear two hats. They may be your mom and dad but they are also "grandma" and "grandpa." Once your divorce was final, something called a normal routine was reestablished. The announcement of a new marriage disrupts the routine and conjures up a whole new set of concerns for the grandchildren.

Loyalty conflicts can arise with your parents as well as your children. Lil said, "I'm not finding it easy to accept Sarah as my daughter–in–law because I'm so fond of my son's first wife and I really miss her."

When your husband–to–be's first wife has a good relationship with his parents, it's an adjustment for them to send her holiday cards that say "to a special friend" and put "to a dear daughter–in–law" on your card. And, you may be faced with a period of cringing when your parents innocently refer to your new husband by your first husband's name.

Parents learn that they can nurture the old relationship just as they nurture the new one. You're not a replacement. As the kids say, "You fit into a new slot."

There may be clear indications that your slot is not a perfect fit. Meg said that her new mother–in–law made it perfectly clear that, "The silver is only to be used by my natural grandchildren." And I think that for every mean grandmother, there are three loving ones. For example, Charlotte's new mother–in–law immediately added Charlotte's daughters to her list for holiday cards and gifts.

Many grandparents read Ann Landers and she tells them that second marriages are always complicated when children are involved. Ann Landers advises grandparents to develop a spirit of generosity and even–handedness to see them through. I hope that's what your children's grandparents do.

Alas! Another instance of the triumph of hope over experience.
> — Samuel Johnson

Announcements and Invitations

You can't be formally engaged while you're married to someone else. It is appropriate to wait until legal proceedings for your divorce or legal annulment are completed before you wear an engagement ring or announce your plans to marry. If you plan to have a religious ceremony and need a religious divorce or annulment on top of the civil rulings, it would be in bad taste to make your announcement before these proceedings are finished.

Formal Engagement Announcements

Couples planning encore weddings usually prefer to make their news known informally and privately. If the engagement is announced publicly, the couple usually does it jointly; it is only for first engagements that the bride's parents make the announcement.

As a general rule, you do not send in an announcement to the newspaper unless you or your fiancé are very prominent in the town or city in which you live. In that case, the engagement

You may not get an enthusiastic acceptance from everyone you invite. Heidi said that they did invite her ex-husband's parents "because they are my children's grandparents. They chose not to come because they said they weren't 'into being grandparents.'" Or, others may not feel as comfortable with the invitation as you and your fiancé. Alan said they invited his sister's ex-husband, "So my sister decided that she wouldn't come."

announcement is sent to the society editor as a news event.

There is one consideration, however. If your engagement is a news event, the papers tend to list the names of former spouses and go into details that aren't particularly relevant to your upcoming nuptials. Before you stir up that pot, decide if this how you want to begin your public lives together.

Who's to be Invited?

Encore weddings often have a very small gathering for the ceremony and a larger group for the reception. You will make your guest list for an encore wedding in the same fashion as you did for a first wedding, with two very sensitive additional groups to consider—your children and your former family members.

Children

Parents today have virtually abandoned the destructive old rule that barred children from their encore weddings. Today, we realize that children will adjust to a new family more easily if they are a part of its formation. Therefore, they should always have the option of attending the wedding. The children may decline the invitation but, at least, they'll know they are welcome.

No child should be forced to attend a parent's wedding. In fact, children sometimes do refuse to attend because they are bitter or really dislike the person their parent has chosen to marry. Sometimes they are happy about the marriage but are simply very uncomfortable with the idea of being there.

If your older son or daughter says, "I just don't feel I can," accept his or her decision gracefully. You could respond, "I hope you'll change your mind, but I will accept whatever you decide." Feelings may indeed change as plans are made and the date comes closer. Allow space for a change of mind without a lot of fanfare.

In the case of reluctant younger children, let them off the hook by helping to make other arrangements for them on your wedding day. If you make those arrangements with someone such as a favorite aunt or uncle on your side of the family (instead of your children's other parent), they will still have the alternative of changing their minds—without guilt.

Some parents avoid thinking about the role that their children will play in the wedding. They leave things to work themselves out. This attitude sets the stage for an ex-spouse to make unilateral decisions that nobody feels comfortable about. For instance, one former spouse whisked the children out of town on the wedding day "to protect the children's feelings because they seemed to have been left out." Discuss your plans with your children and their other parent!

Former Family Members

When you make the decision to invite more than the immediate family to the ceremony, you must decide whether or not to include people who were part of your family through your previous marriage. Either position is socially correct.

The question of whether these parents-in-law, or former sisters- or brothers-in-law, are to be invited is one that must be settled according to the unique circumstances of your family. If you are still very close with these family members, you and your fiancé should discuss this first. Consider whether it would create an embarrassing situation with the new family, the children, or the grandchildren.

If you both decide you would like to invite them, then speak with your former family members. If they are thrilled at the prospect of your remarriage and welcome your new spouse as your children's stepparent, there's no reason to exclude them.

One couple I know planned their marriage in just a week! They decided to arrange for a very small, very private wedding at an exclusive local ranch resort. The bride printed announcements for all the many friends and business acquaintances the couple had. She mailed them on the way to her ceremony. Lots of her friends left shocked messages on her answering machine but rallied together and threw the couple a party a few weeks later!

Divorces create sticky situations. When issuing invitations, be prepared to gracefully accept a refusal. Many couples choose to invite former in-laws "because of the grandchildren." The invitations are received by the in-laws as a courtesy they often appreciate. However, in practice, not many of them actually attend.

The Invitation

Usually the small number of people who attend the ceremony are issued an invitation in the form of a personal note. This is the most flattering invitation possible. Use a good quality paper for your invitation. It may be monogrammed paper or formal paper with your name and address.

You would write to your relatives and friends; your fiancé would write to his.

A typical wedding invitation note from the bridegroom would look like this:

A typical note from the bride would look like this:

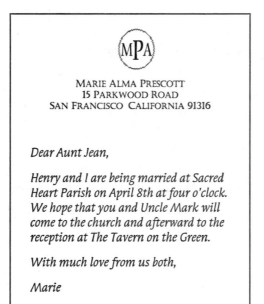

MPA

MARIE ALMA PRESCOTT
15 PARKWOOD ROAD
SAN FRANCISCO CALIFORNIA 91316

Dear Aunt Jean,

Henry and I are being married at Sacred Heart Parish on April 8th at four o'clock. We hope that you and Uncle Mark will come to the church and afterward to the reception at The Tavern on the Green.

With much love from us both,

Marie

Henry James Boden
256 Commonwealth Avenue
Chicago, Illinois 60611

Dear Keith,

Marie Prescott and I are being married at four o'clock on Thursday, the eighth of April. The ceremony will be at Sacred Heart Parish in San Francisco. We hope that you will be able to join us for the ceremony and dinner reception afterwards.

Affectionately yours,

Uncle Henry

Encore Wedding Invitations: A Portfolio of Examples

A handwritten note or a telephone call are preferred for an invitation to the ceremony of an encore wedding. You may have the engravers prepare formal invitations for the reception and for the wedding announcements, if you wish to send them.

However, if the wedding will be a large one and you have your heart set on engraved wedding invitations, there are basic guidelines for wording them. The age of the bride determines how the invitation should be phrased. Young divorcées require one phrasing, older ones, another.

In this instance, a young divorcée is a woman under thirty years old who is entering her second marriage at a time when many of her friends may be planning their first wedding. Her first marriage was of short duration and she does not have children. A mature divorcée is a woman over thirty years old who has been independent since her divorce. Her first marriage was either short or long in duration and she may or may not have children.

Bride is a young divorcée. Parents of the bride issue invitation.

These invitations may be sent by your parents and read the same as the invitations to a first wedding. The only difference is that you will include your last name. The name on the invitation will be the one you are currently using. If you have dropped your ex–husband's name, use your own first, middle and maiden names —

Marie Alma Prescott

— or your maiden name with your ex-husband's last name, as in this example.

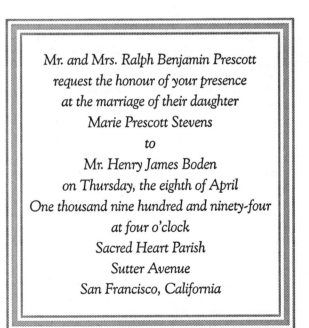

Mr. and Mrs. Ralph Benjamin Prescott
request the honour of your presence
at the marriage of their daughter
Marie Prescott Stevens
to
Mr. Henry James Boden
on Thursday, the eighth of April
One thousand nine hundred and ninety-four
at four o'clock
Sacred Heart Parish
Sutter Avenue
San Francisco, California

Bride is a mature divorcée. Bride and groom issue the invitation

If you have been independent since your divorce, you would generally issue your own invitations. This bride resumed using her maiden name after her divorce. Using a touch of formality, the invitation might look like this example.

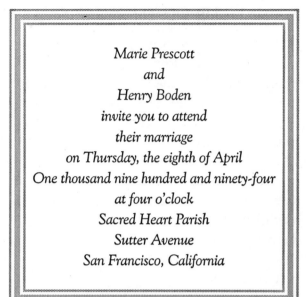

Marie Prescott
and
Henry Boden
invite you to attend
their marriage
on Thursday, the eighth of April
One thousand nine hundred and ninety-four
at four o'clock
Sacred Heart Parish
Sutter Avenue
San Francisco, California

Here is a variation of phrasing. Most divorced women prefer "Ms." or no title. This bride continued to use her husband's name after the divorce but dropped the title.

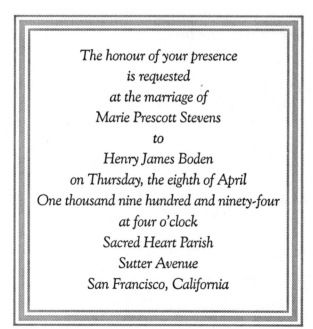

The honour of your presence
is requested
at the marriage of
Marie Prescott Stevens
to
Henry James Boden
on Thursday, the eighth of April
One thousand nine hundred and ninety-four
at four o'clock
Sacred Heart Parish
Sutter Avenue
San Francisco, California

Adult children of the bride issue the invitation.

The names of your offspring are listed in age from oldest to youngest. The bride's name will be in whatever format she is currently using. In this example, they do not use titles.

> Ms. Victoria Ann Stevens
> Ms. Ellen Konah Stevens
> Mr. and Mrs. Parker James Boden
> Ms. Sarah Harrison Boden
> request the honour of your presence
> at the marriage of their parents
> Ms. Marie Prescott Stevens
> to
> Mr. Henry James Boden
> on Thursday, the eighth of April
> One thousand nine hundred and ninety-four
> at four o'clock
> Sacred Heart Parish
> Sutter Avenue
> San Francisco, California

> Victoria Ann Stevens
> Ellen Konah Stevens
> request the honour of your presence
> at the marriage of their mother
> Marie Prescott Stevens
> to
> Henry James Boden
> on Thursday, the eighth of April
> One thousand nine hundred and ninety-four
> at four o'clock
> Sacred Heart Parish
> Sutter Avenue
> San Francisco, California

Adult children of both the bride and groom issue the invitation.

The bride's children are listed before the bridegroom's children. When there are several children involved, their names are given in age, from oldest to youngest, within each family. Note that they did use titles.

There may be an additional charge for printing invitations that are quite lengthy.

Invitations to the Reception

The ceremony is frequently private for an encore wedding. A large reception party may follow. A formal reception invitation, the size of a standard wedding invitation, is sent to all the guests. Insert a small ceremony card, the size of a standard reception card, or handwritten note for guests who are invited to both.

There are many options for phrasing wedding invitations. Once you have made a decision to move outside the realm of the strictly formal invitation, you have space to become creative.

Bride is a young divorcée. Parents of the bride issue the reception invitation.

This invitation looks like a traditional wedding invitation. The bride's name is in whatever form she is currently using.

Mr. and Mrs. Ralph Benjamin Prescott
request the pleasure of your company
at the wedding reception of their daughter
Marie Prescott Stevens
and
Mr. Henry James Boden
on Thursday, April eighth
at half after five o'clock
Wellington Place
San Francisco, California

Bride and bridegroom are mature. Bride and groom issue the invitation.

Mature couples, over thirty years old, usually extend their own invitation to the reception. It looks like an invitation to a formal party. Titles "Mr." and "Ms." are optional. This bride in this example resumed using her maiden name.

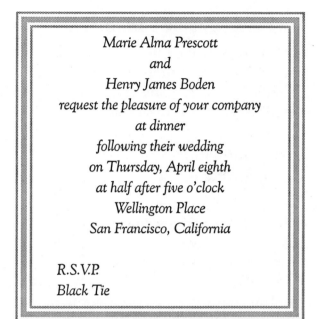

> Marie Alma Prescott
> and
> Henry James Boden
> request the pleasure of your company
> at dinner
> following their wedding
> on Thursday, April eighth
> at half after five o'clock
> Wellington Place
> San Francisco, California
>
> R.S.V.P.
> Black Tie

The Wedding Announcement

It is perfectly correct to send as many engraved announcements of the marriage as you wish. The variations in family circumstances, names, and titles are the same as those described for ceremony and reception invitations in this chapter and for first weddings described earlier in this book.

Parents announce the marriage of a young divorcée.

When announcements are sent by a young bride's parents, the form is just like that of a first wedding announcement. Since they are intended to give information, you may include the name of the groom's parents. Such an announcement would look like this example.

Divorcée and her new husband announce their marriage.

The bride uses her former husband's last name if she wishes to, or her maiden name if she resumed using her maiden name after the divorce. The "Mr." and "Ms." titles are optional.

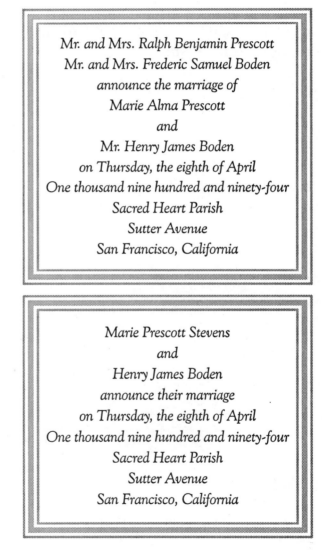

Mr. and Mrs. Ralph Benjamin Prescott
Mr. and Mrs. Frederic Samuel Boden
announce the marriage of
Marie Alma Prescott
and
Mr. Henry James Boden
on Thursday, the eighth of April
One thousand nine hundred and ninety-four
Sacred Heart Parish
Sutter Avenue
San Francisco, California

Marie Prescott Stevens
and
Henry James Boden
announce their marriage
on Thursday, the eighth of April
One thousand nine hundred and ninety-four
Sacred Heart Parish
Sutter Avenue
San Francisco, California

A Sense of Humor

Sometimes encore couples decide to sit back, relax, and have some fun with the encore wedding. This philosophy is more likely to occur if the bride has already had a "dream wedding," and it is more than likely when couples are tying the knot for the third or fourth time. Karen told me that she and Ray were each marrying for the third time. They sent handwritten notes inviting guests to "Act III, Scene I, Prologue."

Mary said that she and her soon-to-be stepbrother issued the invitations for their parents in a traditional format. At the bottom, they had printed:

> *"Please—as we are combining two households*
> *and already have two of everything—no gifts.*
> *Reception and garage sale immediately following."*

And, of course, who could ever forget receiving this wedding invitation.

Michelle "Once is enough" Sullivan
and
Bradford "I'll never marry again" Lodge
invite you to join them
in "eating their words"
on Saturday, the eighth of June
Black Rock Yacht Club
Camden, Maine

The Wedding Day

A wedding between a man and a woman who are well acquainted not only with life, but with each other, can be a very festive occasion. Before starting to plan your ceremony and festivities, find out about any regulations or restrictions, legal and religious, on your remarriage.

Meet with the officiant you would like to have perform the ceremony. Any variations in the rites or number of participants in the total ceremony will need approval. You will have your own ideas for personalizing your encore wedding and the officiant may have some additional suggestions.

Ceremony Size and Type

Since this is an encore wedding for you and your fiancé, it is best to have a semiformal or informal wedding. It may take place in your home or garden, a church or chapel, a hotel or club. Encore wedding ceremonies often take place during the daytime and may be performed by any one of many authorized officiants.

It is also very nice to have your children stand as your witnesses if the children:

- Are twelve years old or older.

- Understand the significance of the wedding ritual.

- Are very happy about the new union.

Joanne told me that she and Elliott had a home wedding with 20 people attending. "We invited our families and our two closest friends."

Bruce said, "Jill and I had a sunset ceremony at the club. Afterwards, there were cocktails, lots of hors d'oeuvres, and a wedding cake."

"Our wedding was very small. We had a Justice of the Peace, our mothers and fathers, the children, and one friend each," Ray contributed.

Civil ceremonies, often the choice for remarriages, are ideal for small informal weddings. If you choose a religious ceremony, it should also be small and include only family and your very closest friends.

If you feel that you got cheated the last time and are determined to have a big wedding with all the trimmings, go ahead. That's one of the advantages of being a grown-up. You can disregard all sensible advice. Just plan the extravaganza with an air of humor about it. Then, your guests won't feel that they have to keep a straight face.

Acquired Tastes

When you have been married before, you may be looking for some adventure with this new wedding. I've heard many stories from couples who decided to scrap the idea of a traditional wedding of any size. They "just go somewhere and get married."

Jeanne and David said, "We planned a vacation and eloped while we were away. Of course, our children and parents knew about our plans beforehand. We sent announcement postcards to our friends."

Some couples who have children from a previous marriage choose to celebrate their weddings with the family together at the honeymoon spot. It allows the children to feel included and provides time for both halves of the extended families to be together.

Mary and Barry took the children to Florida for vacation. "We invited all of our parents to come down and join us for the ceremony. We were married in the chapel near my folks' retirement home."

Members of the Wedding Party— Honor Attendants

Your time for a grand parade of bridesmaids has passed. As witnesses, you will have a maid or matron of honor and your groom will have a best man. If ushers are needed, they will seat guests and then be seated themselves. They do not stand at the altar.

The honor attendants for an encore wedding are most often members of the bridal couple's families. Brothers and sisters are a popular choice.

Some people consider it indelicate to have as attendants children whose other parent is still living. If you do want to include your children in this manner, discuss your wishes with your former spouse first, especially if the children live with him or her. When the children are close to both parents, both mother and father need to work together to assuage any feelings of conflicting loyalty. Extend your invitation to the children only after this parent–to–parent conversation has taken place. Then invite the children to join you in celebrating a new beginning.

An account of a wedding was reported in *The New York Times*. The maid of honor was eleven, the best man, thirteen, and the usher, eight. All three were described as "model attendants at their mother's second marriage." Later that year, the children attended their father at his second marriage. "I'm getting the hang of it now." remarked the thirteen–year–old.

"The kids planned our wedding," according to Linda and Edwin. "After the ceremony, we all went out for Chinese food. Edwin's ex-wife didn't take the boys after our ceremony because she had a date," Linda added. That's life!

Terry said that he and Lauren were married in the church hall. "We had the ceremony and the reception in the same room at our church."

Roseanne's mother spoke about her daughter's lawn wedding. "I actually preferred her outdoor wedding. There were no walls for me to bounce off of!"

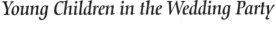

Young Children in the Wedding Party

Although encore weddings do not usually include lots of attendants, exceptions are made for your children. However many children there are may be added to the two basic attendants—maid or matron of honor and best man.

Young daughters or granddaughters may be junior bridesmaids or flower girls. Young sons or grandsons may be junior ushers or ring bearers.

Missy was becoming a stepmother to two teenagers and a little girl. "Andrew and I asked them to participate as junior bridesmaids and our flower girl." Missy included them in the wedding plans, allowing them to choose the fabric and colors for their dresses.

Louis said that he asked his six-year-old stepson-to-be if he would like to be the ring bearer. "The priest had Ian stand next to him during the ceremony. Ian was bursting with pride."

Depending upon their ages and degree of enthusiasm for the wedding, the children may choose to attend the guest book, light special candles, read a poem or scripture passage, sing a song, help decorate the ceremony or the reception site, assist in holding a floral arbor, or simply be part of the excitement of dressing up for the wedding.

One wedding consultant Kathy told me about a wedding where the oldest daughter, Gayle, was just a few years younger than the bride-to-be. Rather than being a member of the wedding party, she finally chose to read a poem that she wrote about her hope that her father would find everlasting happiness in this marriage. Kathy said there wasn't a dry eye in the church.

When young children participate, look to relatives to help guide them through the festivities. Ask a grandparent, aunt, uncle, or cousin to provide the necessary transportation and supervision for youngsters, as well as to help them get dressed and calm their jitters. A large part of your relative's job will be to give the children hugs, as needed, throughout the day.

If your children do not want to actively participate in the ceremony, make sure that they are escorted to the seats of honor reserved for them in the first few rows, near the officiant.

The Aisle

When your wedding party is small—that is, you do not have your children serving as bridesmaids, ushers, flower girls, or ring bearers—you do not usually have a processional up the aisle.

The bride and groom, together with their attendants, emerge from either side of the ceremony site and meet in front of the officiant. This is appropriate for both a religious and a civil ceremony.

Family circumstances and the limitations of the site will be your determining factors.

As for the music, the symbolism is bad in Wagner's Lohengrin, which gave us the golden oldie, "Here Comes the Bride". Has no one noticed that Lohengrin leaves Elsa in the third act?

"Giving Away" the Bride

Once given away in a wedding ceremony, that's it for a bride. It is not customary to be given away for an encore wedding. I think it's far fetched to think that the father of a young bride in America has had much say in disposing of her hand. Giving away a grown woman is ridiculous.

Since the line, "Who giveth this woman . . . ?" is in most wedding ceremony rites, be sure to weed it out during the rehearsal.

An "Acceptance Ceremony" is a nice substitute for this portion of the ritual. It is an opportunity for family members to say a few words about accepting the new spouse into their family. If you like

There are a number of ways for a bride to navigate the aisle. She may:

- Walk down the aisle alone.
- Walk with her groom.
- Walk with her father.
- Walk with a brother.
- Walk in with a son.

Karen described her family walk this way. "My father walked me three-quarters of the way down the aisle. My 10-year old son, Martin, met us and the three of us walked the rest of the way together."

Miriam laughed. "This was the third marriage for each of us. We don't have any children. Matt and I walked down the aisle together while the organ played, *'I have often walked down this street before . . .'*"

If you know you want to add a little something to the ceremony but don't know exactly what, there are resources available. Consider looking at:

🌱 Anthologies under "love" and "marriage."

🌱 A Bible concordance that lists verses by subject.

🌱 New Age literature.

🌱 Scripture selections.

🌱 Song lyrics that are read, not sung.

🌱 A hymn sung by guests.

🌱 Poetry books.

this idea, select relatives from each side ahead of time so they have an opportunity to prepare what they wish to say.

The Personalized Ceremony

Almost all religions and officiants now allow some variations in the ceremony. Before you begin to think about additions, read through the standard form and do some discreet editing by omitting details that you find inappropriate. Typical examples are such items as "obeying" and "giving away."

Traditional ceremonies, civil or religious, express hopes and ideals. Major alterations that delve into deep philosophical concepts—understood only by you and your groom—are not in good taste. The ceremony rites are intended to apply generally to the religious and social occasion, not to enter the realm of your private relationship.

As you begin your search for personal additions, remember to keep speaking parts to a minimum. This is especially true if you plan to memorize the words. You cannot count on remaining calm, cool and collected throughout the ceremony. In fact, plan to give the officiant a typed copy of your parts so you have a prompter nearby.

There are some portions of the service that we all take for granted. One of these is the response to "Will you take this man/woman to be your wedded husband/wife?" Here's a test. Which is the correct response, "I do," or "I will," or "I shall"?

The answer is, there is no right or wrong response. "I do" is the most frequently used. However, each option is acceptable in a marriage ceremony that is personalized. The Episcopal Prayer Book uses the "I will" response when the marriage is initially celebrated in the church. The "I do" response is used when the Episcopal ceremony is blessing a civil marriage. In all circumstances, "I shall" is the correct response for grammatical purists.

The Day We All Got Married

The parents' vows to each other may be followed by a family vow or prayer of family unity with each member adding a phrase.

"Children often experience anticipation and excitement before the wedding starts, but, afterwards, they're confused and feel left out," says Dr. Roger Coleman, a Christian church (Disciples of Christ) minister.

Dr. Coleman is the author of "Celebrating the New Family," a ceremony booklet for including children in the wedding service when parents marry following divorce or death of a spouse. During the ceremony, a "Family Medallion" disk is given to each child—symbolizing the new family. A reading on the importance of children is then given, followed by a prayer for the children. According to Dr. Coleman, through this gesture the parents are saying, "We care for you and you have a special place in our lives."

The Family Medallion has three raised circles on its face. Two represent the marriage union while the third symbolizes the importance of children in the marriage. It represents family love in the same way the wedding ring symbolizes conjugal love. Contact Clergy Services, (800) 237–1922, for more information.

For their new wedding rings, I have noticed that encore brides often prefer other gems to diamonds. Colored stones such as a ruby, amethyst, sapphire, or emerald are very popular for engagement rings and wedding bands. However, nothing beats the simplicity and beauty of a plain gold wedding band.

The idea of presenting a special gift to each child is not new. I heard many ideas for mementoes. Couples gave children things they could begin to enjoy immediately such as cameras, tape recorders, and engraved jewelry.

"Dennis and I gave our boys heavy gold initial rings," Rosalie said.

Patrick and Arlene chose gifts that could be part of future family rituals. "We got silver loving cups for all of the children. They had our wedding date engraved on them and the cups were used for all future special occasions."

"We had a very small family wedding. Our guests gave the children wedding gifts instead of giving them to us," another couple said.

"Children often experience anticipation and excitement before the wedding starts, but, afterwards, they're confused and feel left out," says Dr. Roger Coleman.

"One grandmother had a list of 'Do's' and 'Don't's' for my second wedding. About the cake, she said, 'No bride and groom on the top.'"

The Reception

Although your wedding ceremony may be small and intimate, do plan any size or style wedding reception your hearts desire. Neither the bride's nor the groom's marital history have any effect on this party. In fact, having a large reception is a nice way of including friends in your celebration.

Use traditional party etiquette for your hosting responsibilities. Greet your guests as they arrive. You will not have a formal receiving line. If each guest is also invited to the ceremony, you may also reverse tradition and stand by the door of the ceremony site and greet guests as they arrive for the service.

All newlyweds should have a wedding cake. It is certainly proper for an encore wedding. This is the time to cater to special style and flavor whims. Chocolate cake is a favorite the second time around.

Ellen said that she and Clifford made a joint decision about the cake. "I chose a chocolate cake with chocolate frosting. Cliff got to choose the top decoration. He picked Superman and Wonder Woman!"

You may still have first wedding customs such as toasting with champagne, cutting the wedding cake and feeding each other the first piece, and having a first dance. Celebratory toasts are a very important part of this celebration.

Laura said she still gets teary when she thinks about the toast made by her oldest brand-new stepdaughter, "We're glad you're going to be our other mom."

It is not generally considered appropriate to toss the bouquet or garter or to throw rice at an encore wedding. Uncooked rice was traditionally tossed as a symbol of fertility for youthful brides and grooms. Because it may be a health hazard for birds, many reception sites specifically forbid its use for weddings. Rose petals and bubbles are a wonderful alternative and perfectly acceptable for encore marriages.

The Delayed Reception

Encore couples frequently decide to throw a reception party several weeks or months after the nuptials.

These parties may also be given by family or friends in honor of the newlyweds. They may be casual family get-togethers or formal affairs. Invitations may be by phone or by printed invitation depending upon the event.

Some couples have a celebration party to welcome friends to their new home. This is usually done after the two families have combined their households and have completed most of the requisite redecorating to make the new place feel like it belongs to both of them.

Becky told me that she and Michael had a theme party. "We eloped while on a vacation during the summer. That fall we invited friends to a sing-along musical program and buffet supper. Our invitations were printed on paper shaped like a grand piano. We had wedding cake for dessert."

The Honeymoon

The brides and bridegrooms offering ideas for this book also had comments about honeymoons when you have children. With the exception of those few couples who took wedding trips with the whole family in tow, the overwhelming response was, "Include children in anything and everything except the honeymoon."

Whatever you decide to do, have fun.

Gary felt that the entire honeymoon should be without children. "Celebrate your return with a date for the whole family. Do something that everyone will enjoy such as going to the theater or a sporting event."

Dolores advised, "Keep the honeymoon short if the children are young. As an alternative, have them join you for the latter part of the trip."

Marie & Henry's Story

Couples of all ages and with many different combinations of children and stepchildren responded to my request for information about planning an encore wedding. Couples planning remarriages had very different stories to tell from first-timers.

Marie Prescott and Henry Boden dealt with many of the issues described in this book. In reading their story, you will see the questions that arose for them and how they were handled. And you will notice that in planning this remarriage, the couple spent a lot of time talking about how to merge their two families and very little time about the wedding ceremony and the reception. The complexities of combining kids, careers, in-laws, finances, friends, residences, belongings and personal idiosyncrasies take precedence over the more "frivolous" etiquette questions that so confound first-timers. Here is Marie and Henry's story based upon my long interviews with them.

COMBINING TWO FAMILIES INTO ONE

Marie and Henry had each been divorced for about two years at the time they met. They were both in their late 40's when they married. Between them, they had four children, ranging in ages from sixteen to twenty-four.

Marie's two daughters, Victoria and Ellen, were living with her at the time she met Henry. The girls were eighteen and sixteen years old, respectively, when their mother remarried.

Henry has a daughter, Sarah, and a married son, Parker. His children were twenty-two and twenty-four years old, respectively, at the time of their father's remarriage. Sarah had been making her home with her father while she saved money for her own apartment. Parker and his wife lived in another city.

SHARING TIME, FORGING BONDS

Marie and Henry worked hard at getting to know each other's children even before their marriage. In fact, they describe themselves as a bit aloof from most social activities: "We'd really rather spend time with our kids."

"During our dating days, we planned activities with each, and sometimes all, of the children," Marie said. Romance for this couple flourished in the midst of college hunting, music recitals, orthodontist appointments, and going on outings with a bunch of teenagers. "I don't think you could call this a formal engagement period," Marie laughed.

"Our first all-together activity was a holiday ski vacation which included our four children and my son's girlfriend," Henry reminisced. Other activities included the theater, museums, and amusement parks. They spent portions of holidays both separately and together. Activities with the children involved coordinating everyone's busy schedules. "No easy job!" they both commented.

The couple also took time to get to know each other's circle of friends and to make new ones together. "We have maintained separate friends and developed new ones who share our interests in travel, skiing, and sailing," they both told me. Since it doesn't happen too often in remarriages, they are particularly happy that Marie's best friend's husband and Henry have become close.

MAKING THE DECISION TO MARRY

Marie and Henry were each comfortable with single life. Jobs, finances, social life, and relationships with their families were all quite fulfilling. They enjoyed their own solitude as well as sharing a number of similar interests. The idea of marriage evolved naturally. "We didn't need each other to create our own happiness or to provide caretaking," Henry told me, "life was just better and nicer when we were together."

How to relate to the children after they got married was a frequent topic of conversation. From the beginning, they made a commitment that primary parenting responsibilities (emotional, financial, and disciplinary) would stay with the biological parent. "We would be friends, confidants, helpers, and emotional support to each other's children, but not authority figures," Marie said.

"We agreed that we would each be

responsible for our own relationships with the children," Henry added. "We would not jump in and take sides or try to 'fix it' when a problem came up with the other's children."

Marie and Henry also decided how they would manage the circle of friends and family they each brought to their union. "We both retained responsibility for relationships with our own extended families," Marie explained. This included telephone calls and written correspondence as well as birthday and holiday gifts and cards. "But, when I send my brother a birthday card, I do sign it from Marie and me," Henry said.

After much soul-searching, they agreed to live in Henry's new house and rent Marie's condominium. This was not Henry's marital home so the only skeletons in the closet were memories of his bachelor days. Minor repairs such as repainting and wallpapering were scheduled before they installed Marie's furniture into his nearly empty house. They have a running joke about his marrying her for her furniture. "That may be partly true," Henry says while laughing, "but, it would have been cheaper to rent furniture!"

They reached a mutually agreeable standard of neatness and cleanliness for their home and shared responsibility for maintaining it. The division of labor was somewhat traditional. Marie managed the interior; Henry took care of the yard. Marie cooked; Henry cleaned up the dishes; and "We both take out the garbage." They decided to use separate bathrooms to avoid bickering over whose turn it was to clean them.

Following her divorce, Marie had resumed using her maiden name. "I really didn't want to change my name again," Marie explained. "Henry didn't see my taking his name as an obligation on my part and felt he could handle the 'separate names' scene. It has only taken our parents two or three years to get used to addressing our envelopes correctly. Some of our friends still don't, however."

Even first names can be confusing, the couple found. "When you've each been previously married for a long time, you have to develop a sense of humor about occasionally being called by the ex's name," Henry told me with a twinkle in his eye. "We decided we'd keep a running list of 'You owe me one' whenever it happened. In five years, we've done pretty well. The list isn't too long!"

A PRENUPTIAL AGREEMENT?

"Neither one of us were wealthy—we still aren't—but since we both have children, assets, and liabilities, I guess we were prime candidates for a prenuptial agreement," Henry said, turning to more serious topics. "That's true," added Marie, "and we talked about all of those issues and how we'd like to handle them but we didn't draw up legal papers."

This couple talked over virtually every foreseeable issue before getting married. They both felt comfortable with the understandings they had arrived at, therefore they chose not to draw up a formal prenuptial agreement. While it may have been an appropriate decision in this particular case, my personal belief is that most remarrying couples with children, assets, liabilities, and responsibilities should strongly consider drawing up a written agreement.

BUSINESS DETAILS

I asked Marie and Henry how they handled specific financial issues. For instance, what about insurances for life, property, health, and umbrella coverage. Business details can become very complicated in remarriages. Though not "etiquette" in the traditional sense, these matters need to be dealt with in a responsible, systematic way before the wedding.

"Existing life insurance policies remained with our children as beneficiaries," Marie explained. "Any new policies, through work or private coverage, are for each other. We each continue to maintain insurance on the property we own separately. We wanted property acquired after the marriage to be jointly owned

and insured. And we spent weeks researching and comparing umbrella coverage, health, and car insurance for ourselves and our children."

PLANNING FINANCIAL TOGETHERNESS—OR SEPARATENESS

I wanted to know how they decided to manage everyday finances. They told me that since they each already had their own credit histories and cards as well as individual bank and brokerage accounts, they agreed to maintain them as usual. They also agreed to pay for their own expenses related to children, insurance premiums, repairs and maintenance of property individually owned, and personal expenses for clothing and gifts. Joint household expenses such as cleaning, groceries, entertainment and vacations were paid for in a flexible manner according to ability to pay. And they both contributed to the cost of their wedding!

THE WEDDING

"When we finally announced our decision to get married, not one of the kids was surprised," Henry said. "In fact, they said they had already told their friends." "We told our parents first," Marie added, "then we took all of the children out for dinner and explained our plans. And then we each called our exes to break the news."

"We're the same faith so we knew we wanted a church ceremony. We had informal counseling sessions with the minister and made plans for a service in June that would be attended by just the children and our parents," Henry said.

Marie supplied the details. "Parker was his dad's best man. Sarah wrote a poem that she read during the service. Vicky and Ellen were my co-maids of honor. My parents and Henry's mom were our only ceremony guests. I wore a pastel green silk dress with flowers in my hair. The girls each wore a flowered dress—they weren't identical dresses. Henry and Parker wore dark suits. It was all very pretty but relaxed and informal."

"I didn't walk down the aisle," Marie said, "we just entered the front of the chapel together from a side door. And we didn't make very many changes in the prayer book service except to leave out the parts about 'giving away' and 'obeying.' And, we added a segment that spoke about family unity and each of the children having a very special place in our new family."

The couple arranged a reception party at the town beach club to celebrate with their friends. There was a buffet supper, dance band, and a three-layer rectangular sheet cake with flowers on top that was decorated like a wedding cake. "We had many champagne toasts," Henry said, "some of them were really funny—and Marie and I danced the first dance together, but, other than that, it was just a typical cocktail party with live music."

I wanted to know how they invited their guests. "Well, for the wedding, we just spoke with our parents and the children," Marie answered. "We sent formal party invitations for the cocktail party. Our guests didn't know it was a wedding reception until they got there and we said, 'Surprise!'"

Marie and Henry decided not to send formal announcements to acquaintances who lived far away. Marie wrote one of those chatty Christmas letters that included their big news and their new address. And they arranged to get together with close friends who could not come to the reception party.

LIFE SETTLES DOWN

Adjustment after the wedding took a bit of time even with all the planning and work Marie and Henry put in beforehand.

In the beginning, Marie's girls would periodically comment, "We're glad you're happy BUT it sure seems that you don't have as much time for us anymore." Marie admitted, "Even though I knew better, I assumed that just because the girls really liked Henry they would settle easily into the new routine. Fortunately, they had no trouble verbalizing their problem adjusting from 'just the three of us' to 'just the five of us.' Henry and I both learned that it was important to spend time with our children separately as well as together."

"What the children call you says a lot about the closeness of the relationship," Henry noted. "Vicky and Ellen refer to me as their 'step-Pop' and sometimes they address me by an affectionate name they coined— 'Hank-O'." My daughter calls Marie 'Mama-Two.' Parker still introduces Marie as 'my father's wife.' I know this makes her feel like an outsider but I think it has more to do with maintaining loyalty to his mother than any negative feelings about Marie. Parker is very close to his mother and she has not remarried. But, no, I have not discussed this with him."

Marie agreed with Henry's observations. Then she laughed and said, "The kids let us know, in little ways, that they think of us as a family. They've already put dibs on antique household items, jewelry and my fur coat—for when we make up the distribution list that goes with our wills!"

Index

"S" after page numbers indicates a sidebar on that page.

Wilshire Publications

Other Titles Published by Wilshire Publications

All About Him - A Personal Reference from the Man in My Life, Beverly Clark and Marcella L. Jaegle, 1995 ISBN 0-93408-11-5

All About Her - A Personal Reference from the Woman in My Life, Beverly Clark and Marcella L. Jaegle, 1995 ISBN 0-934081-19-7

Planning A Wedding to Remember, Beverly Clark, 1986 ISBN 0-934081-09-3

Weddings: A Celebration, Beverly Clark, 1996 ISBN 0-934081-14-X

Wedding Memories, Beverly Clark, 1990 ISBN 0-934081-05-0

Showers - The Complete Guide to Hosting a Perfect Bridal or Baby Shower, Beverly Clark, 1989 ISBN 0-934081-05-0

I Marry You Because, Peter McWilliams, 1995 ISBN 0-934081-15-8

A Special Day for You, Coloring Book, 1996 ISBN 0-934081-12-3

Other Books Written by Margorie Engel

Divorce Help Sourcebook, Margorie Engel, Ph.D. 1994 ISBN 0-8103-9480-4, Published by Visible Ink Press and Gale Research

Divorce Decisions Workbook: A Planning and Action Guide, Margorie Engel, Ph.D. ISBN 0-07-019572-2, Published by McGraw-Hill, Inc.

Beverly Clark Collection

Bridal accessories

All About Her

All About Him

Fill in the blanks, practical and romantic reference guidebooks to and from your mate.

A Special Day For you!

8½" x 11" coloring book with 32 fun–filled pages to color, games to play and puzzles to solve. Includes a box of 4 crayons.

Also available:

Weddings: A Celebration
A pictorial excursion through the world's most exquisite weddings. More than 500 luxurious color photographs feature romantic events from the traditional to the uncommon.

Planning a Wedding to Remember
The nation's best selling planning guide is filled with essential information and hundreds of unique ideas. Includes checklists, worksheets and organizer pockets.

**For additional product information or a store nearest you,
please call 1(800) 888-6866
Website Address: www.beverlyclark.com
E-mail: info@beverlyclark.com**